The Kosher Billionaire's Secret Recipe

STACY COHEN

The Kosher Billionaire's Secret Recipe

STACY COHEN

Art Direction & Fashion Photography by
Amedeo M. Turello

Food Photography by
Quentin Bacon

Design by
Johanna Rossi

Foreword by
Dr. Dean Ornish

Contributing Nutritionist
Dr. Melina Jampolis

ATRIA BOOKS
New York London Toronto Sydney

BEYOND WORDS
PUBLISHING

ATRIA BOOKS

PUBLISHING

A Division of Simon & Schuster, Inc.
1230 Avenue of the Americas
New York, NY 10020

20827 N.W. Cornell Road, Suite 500
Hillsboro, Oregon 97124-9808
503-531-8700 / 503-531-8773 fax
www.beyondword.com

The information contained in this book is intended to be educational.
The author and publishers are in no way liable for any use or misuse of the information.

Project Coordinator: Chethan Ramachandran
Fashion and Lifestyle Photography: Amedeo M. Turello
Food Photography: Quentin Bacon
Book Production and Layout: Johanna Rossi and Amedeo M. Turello
Digital Retouching: Steve Navarre
Beauty Director: Roberto Rosini
Fashion Editor and Styling: Rosanna Trinchese
Stylist: Gaia Giovetti
Hair Styling: Roberto Rosini, Clifford Hashimoto, Cassie Chapman
Makeup: Rosanna Trinchese, Greta Weatherby
Recipe Coordinator: Peter Berley
Food Stylist: George Dolce, Elisabet der Nederlanden
Floral Arrangements and Food Props: Joe Mayer and Chris White
Flowers: Brandon Espanosa
Heart Doctor and Adviser: Dr. Dean Ornish
Nutritionist: Dr. Melina Jampolis
Master Sommelier: Catherine Fallis
Videographer: Sir Less

First Atria Books/Beyond Words hardcover edition September 2007

ATRIA BOOKS and colophon are trademarks of Simon & Schuster, Inc.
Beyond Words Publishing is a division of Simon & Schuster, Inc.

For more information about special discounts for bulk purchases, please contact Simon & Schuster Special Sales at 1-800-456-6798 or business@simonandschuster.com.

Printed and bound in England by Butler and Tanner

10 9 8 7 6 5 4 3 2 1

Library of Congress Control Number: 2007920784

ISBN-13: 978-1-58270-169-1
ISBN-10:   1-58270-169-5

The corporate mission of Beyond Words Publishing, Inc.: *Inspire to Integrity*

to my adoring husband for all the love he has given me

"You must do the thing you think you cannot do."

—ELEANOR ROOSEVELT

Contents

"If you have built castles in the air,
your work need not be lost; there is where they should be.
Now put foundations under them."

—Henry David Thoreau

Foreword

Stacy Cohen and her husband are philanthropists who helped support the research that my colleagues and I conducted at the nonprofit Preventive Medicine Research Institute. We demonstrated that the simple choices that we make each day in our lives—what we eat, how we respond to stress, whether or not we smoke, how much we exercise, and the quality of our relationships—make a powerful difference in our health and well-being. We found that a plant-based, low-fat, whole-foods diet, along with stress management techniques, moderate exercise, and support groups, could reverse the progression of even severe coronary heart disease. We also measured significant improvements in prostate cancer, diabetes, high blood pressure, depression, and obesity.

Kosher food is traditionally among the least heart-healthy—often loaded with saturated fat, total fat, and cholesterol, in foods such as cream cheese, herring, chopped liver, tongue, eggs. And, too, kosher food is not usually known for culinary inspiration. In this book, however, Stacy provides a spectrum of choices—from healthier and more creative versions of low-fat, delicious vegetarian kosher food to the most indulgent.

Billionaires can afford to eat anything they want. So why would Stacy and her husband choose to eat only kosher foods? Why would anyone choose to limit their diet if they could afford to eat almost anything? Why not do everything you want to do? When you can afford almost anything, it's important to have some self-imposed limitations. Choosing not to do something that we otherwise could do helps define who we are, reminds us that we have free will, freedom of choice. Only when we can say "no" we are free to say "yes."

All religions have dietary restrictions, though they may differ in the details. Whatever the intrinsic benefit in eating or avoiding certain foods, just the act of choosing not to eat or not to do something that we otherwise might be able to do—as in keeping kosher—helps to make our lives more sacred, more special, more disciplined. In this context, what we choose to eat—and not eat—can nourish our souls as well as our bodies.

I've been mostly vegetarian for more than thirty years. Those who are carnivores may be interested to learn that the standards of cleanliness for handling and processing meat are generally higher in facilities certified as kosher than what is required by the United States Department of Agriculture. In addition to cleanliness, the values of being kosher are also about being compassionate. The more mystical traditions warn that the fear and anger present when an animal is slaughtered in inhumane ways may find their way into the hearts of those who eat them.

We may choose to follow the restrictions of our own religion or tradition not simply to please God but rather to experience God. We begin to heal our separation from God and from one another at a time when our world is increasingly polarized and cynical. Each healthy, compassionate, loving meal reminds us that our lives can be an endless gift to ourselves and to others.

—Dean Ornish, M.D.

How to Use This Book

In writing this book, I want to offer you, the reader, two things: an inside look at the fabulous, exciting, and healthy kosher life that I have created, and the opportunity for you to create the same glorious existence for yourself, no matter who you are and where or how you live. At first, this celebrity lifestyle may seem unattainable to you, but it really isn't: your jet may be something you aspire to, your fine art collection may have been drawn by your five-year-old, your travels may take you around the block instead of to Monaco, and the Christian Louboutin mules that line your closet may be wishful thinking. So exactly how can you live this sort of action-packed, magnificent way of life without all the slightly decadent external trappings and still have it be spectacular? Simple: by understanding and following my Kosher Billionaire's Secret Recipe, seeing how it works, and then applying it to every single facet of the way you live.

It's easy, and it will change your life forever!

Stacy Cohen

What Will
The Kosher Billionaire's Secret Recipe Teach You?

How to achieve inner peace by living the good life
How to enjoy healthful gourmet kosher meals and not feel deprived—instead, feel satisfied ... and blessed
How to enjoy sumptuous wines in moderation
How to make regular exercise a joyous part of your day
How to give of yourself in order to help others

The result?
A magnificent inner glow, and stunning outer beauty that will last a lifetime!

In the pages that follow, I will share the three major components of my life that comprise my Kosher Billionaire's Secret Recipe: the way I feed my body, the way I nurture my spiritual side, and the way I care for my heart by always striving to give back to others. Together, these three facets, braided together, create a very big part of my day-to-day life, and they have forever changed the manner in which I live, and even how I think. Each day is more fulfilling, every experience more exciting and thrilling, and life, ultimately, is simply more joyous and healthy; I feel better, I look better, and by adopting my secret recipe, you will too!

As you go through each section of my book you will find that they can be read independently, consecutively, or in any order; so interconnected are the three major components of my Kosher Billionaire's Secret Recipe that the lines often get blurred between them. And that is what makes my glamorous kosher lifestyle so very unique: every facet of it works hand in hand to result in two things—inner peace and outer beauty. When I travel, I enjoy luscious gourmet foods that happen to be kosher and allow me to maintain my spiritual connection on a daily basis. Wherever I go, I meet fascinating people who profoundly affect my outlook on life, and by utilizing my Kosher Billionaire's Secret Recipe, I am able to stay on track wherever I am, and remain healthy, energetic, and contented at the most soulful level.

Best of all, *The Kosher Billionaire's Secret Recipe* is downright fun and deeply exciting! Throughout the book, I will share with you some of the most spectacular, sometimes ever-so-slightly decadent experiences that I've had while enjoying the lavish lifestyle that's taken me to nearly every part of the globe, from Japan to India and beyond. You'll enjoy the sumptuous kosher gourmet recipes, menus, and wines that have become a regular part of my life, and that have enabled me to remain wondrously healthy and spiritually connected, and able to live an action-packed lifestyle without feeling deprived. By reading this book, you'll learn that living the secret recipe lifestyle needn't be a challenge—it can and will be the thrill of a lifetime!

YOU CAN BE A GLAMOROUS JET-SETTER

Living la Dolce Vita, the Kosher Billionaire Way …

Imagine: Dressed in a magnificent La Perla bathing suit and flowing raw silk sarong, you and your high-tech entrepreneur husband board a private helicopter bound for an island paradise. Together, you sit down side by side in the leather seats, slip on the headsets that dull the roar of the chopper blades, and suddenly, you're aloft, being carried gently upward against an azure backdrop dotted by soft, powdery clouds so close you can reach out and touch them. After a short trip, the helicopter eases forward, its nose parting the scrim of white-blue, and as if by magic, a heart-shaped island suddenly appears below you, out of nowhere. Close your eyes, breathe deeply, and imagine for a moment that you have landed amidst the lush, sultry landscape that is French Polynesia. The president of this magnificent island country greets you, and together with his striking Tahitian wife, you are escorted on a tour of a veritable tropical wonderland so dazzling and stunning that it played host to Brigitte Bardot and Roger Vadim as they celebrated their honeymoon. When the exclusive tour is over, you are whisked to another glorious white-sand setting, where you all enjoy a superlative alfresco luncheon featuring fish caught seconds before you arrived, prepared simply and elegantly, and accompanied by a seemingly endless amount of vintage French wines, perfectly matched to the meal and chilled to utter perfection. You watch as the president's wife gently uses the white sand to exfoliate the president's back, and unexpectedly, your magnificent lunch is capped off by the presidential couple swimming in the sun-dappled crystalline waters.

A typical day for a kosher billionaire? Believe it or not, yes. And while most of my days are admittedly not quite as indulgent as the one my husband and I enjoyed in French Polynesia, I make certain that my life, no matter where I am on one of the many luxurious journeys I take each year, is filled with glamour, delicious pleasures, spirituality, philanthropy, and no small amount of what some might consider decadence.

17

In my heart of hearts, I really believe that life is all about living well, taking care of yourself, and giving to others, no matter who you are, where you reside, what you like to eat, what your background is, how you practice your spirituality, or even what you do for a living. The upsides to the kind of lavish existence that my husband and I are lucky enough to enjoy are obvious, and admittedly most of us do strive to live this way at some point in our lives, to experience fascinating and luxurious travel, to eat delectable foods, and to take pleasure and delight in the things with which we surround ourselves. But the downsides are also clear: the regular temptation of large quantities of expertly prepared dishes and fine wines can wreak havoc on our bodies, putting weight on us and literally disconnecting us from any semblance of health, both physical and spiritual. Think about it: how many times have you been surrounded by tantalizing treats in your own home, at parties, or while traveling? Is it possible for you to enjoy luscious foods and wines, and all of the things you love, while staying healthy and connected, and maintaining or even losing weight? Yes! In the coming pages, let me take you on my private aircraft and be your very personal passport to an exciting, delicious, action-packed red carpet ride to life-the good life. It will be an unbelievably fun and thrilling journey suitable for the likes of you, me, and a kosher James Bond. I will share with you my secret tips for enjoying a spectacular, adventure-filled lifestyle while remaining kosher; I will show you how to reach the very top of the mountain, how to be uplifted spiritually, how to look and feel amazing, and how, no matter who you are or where you live, you can make the champagne lifestyle your very own.

I wrote this book for you; you may or may not eat kosher food or live a kosher lifestyle the way my husband and I do, but no matter who we are, we all share the sometimes tricky goal of trying to lose or maintain weight and stay healthy while simultaneously enjoying a fulfilling, satisfying, and slightly decadent lifestyle! Over the years, I have been fortunate enough to learn that good nutrition, health, great food, and a lush lifestyle are not mutually exclusive; gluttony does not translate to healthful living, in the same way that healthful eating doesn't necessarily mean what many of us envision as "health food."

*Is it possible for you to enjoy luscious foods and wines
and all of the things you love, while staying healthy, connected, and maintaining
or even losing weight? In a word, yes.*

We all face daily food challenges, and those of us, like my husband and me, who are either traveling or planning the next adventure, are always confronted with copious amounts of delicious foods that add pleasure and joy to our day-to-day lives. Yet we see no reason to deprive ourselves in the name of health, because we have learned, simply, that we don't have to. Taking care of ourselves is of prime importance, but what we eat in our sumptuous, travel-packed lives is also a vital part of our existence. It gives us pleasure, and what is life without pleasure?

The Kosher Billionaire's Secret Recipe offers a peek into my life, a vicarious look at how I'm able to live a fabulous, healthy, delicious celebrity existence that also happens to be kosher. Every time you pick up this book, you'll step into a pair of imaginary Manolos or sit next to me on my private plane as we travel the world together, eating spectacular foods and drinking magnificent wines.

Whether you actually endeavor to live this splendid lifestyle, or just dream about it, you'll come away with an array of simple but elegant, kosher menus designed for optimal nutrition and weight maintenance or loss, approved by Dr. Melina Jampolis, internationally renowned nutritionist and the Discovery Channel's The Diet Doctor. Based on the classic international cuisines I've enjoyed in my travels around the world from Italy to France and Brazil to India, each menu includes wine pairing suggestions.

By utilizing my special Kosher Billionaire Secret Recipe tips and fabulous life strategies, you will see how easy it is to enjoy a healthy, delicious, and spiritual existence throughout your workweek, on the weekends, at parties, and on vacations. So join me on this voyeuristic look into an action-packed, glamorously stylish kosher life that will change who you are, forever, from the inside out, and will result in a wonderful, natural glow to your outer beauty. Here, you will learn that inner peace and joy are attainable through good, exciting, pleasurable living, which comes down to a few simple things: healthy kosher eating, exercise, joy, and remembering, always, to give back.

My secret recipe will help you be the best you can be in everything you attempt. Come with me as we explore the world together and enjoy its precious gifts.

FEEDING THE BODY

PART I

"Every long journey begins with that first small step."

—STACY COHEN

Use this brilliantly illustrated jewel of a book
to inspire you to dream and to succeed;
or use it as a practical lifestyle book
packed with great menu ideas and style inspiration
from entertaining to fashion and beyond ...

SWEET SUCCESS THE KOSHER WAY

Is it possible to live a glorious, sexy lifestyle and strengthen your spiritual connection while fortifying your body and soul, and reaching the very pinnacle of happiness and success in the process—like a billionaire striving to be the absolute best at what he or she does, and really succeeding at it? Is it really possible to live a wonderfully healthy, gourmet lifestyle filled to the brim with sumptuous feasts, spectacular wines, decadent desserts, travel that takes you to far-off places where the food is as stunning as the scenery and to lose weight without feeling deprived or restricted? It is indeed possible. How do I know this for sure? Because I am here to tell you: I did it. And I want you to know that you can do it too. *The Kosher Billionaire's Secret Recipe* is my revolutionary new program, pairing delicious kosher food with great health and a sexy, jet-setting lifestyle. I offer you my groundbreaking billionaire tips and techniques for achieving success in everyday life, and show you that you can feel amazing and look great, while enjoying more than fifty mouthwatering kosher recipes and delectable desserts never before available anywhere. But first things first: throw away all those nasty diet books and instead, use this brilliantly illustrated jewel of a book to inspire you to dream and to succeed; or use it as a practical lifestyle book packed with great menu ideas and style inspiration for everything from entertaining to fashion and beyond.

But however you use it, stop counting those calories, and come taste the good life with me … you'll never look back. Living a lavish life was not something that I necessarily expected. But great things, as they say, come in packages (and generally only when the timing is right), and for me, they certainly did. I regularly travel the world on my private aircraft, and on any given day, I might be flying off to enjoy a luxurious vacation getaway on the Italian Riviera or Israel, the south of France or Fiji, Greece or the Far East.

Together with my friends and family, I derive great pleasure from sumptuous feasts that seem to go on forever, dessert trays of lovingly prepared, decadent napoleons served on a private terrace overlooking the 8th Arrondissement in Paris, vintage kosher burgundies that flow like the Seine, and all of the fabulous trappings—the clothes, the exotic cars, and the company—that go hand in hand with the opulent lifestyle that I am so very lucky to live … and that you can too! But as delicious as it is, I realized that this extraordinary lifestyle was sometimes resulting in my not watching what I was eating, and I knew that I had to somehow make a change; for me, taking care of myself is an act of deep devotion to the people I love and the causes I support. And there was another small hurdle to overcome as I endeavored to change the way I eat; however I chose to alter my diet, and whatever nutritionist I worked with, we all had to keep in mind that at the very center of my fabulous and glamorous life lies the fact that I am kosher.

KOSHER IS FOR EVERYONE!

Now that I realize that a healthy kosher lifestyle can result in weight loss,
lowered blood pressure, and added energy,
I want to help everyone experience the same terrific benefits.
Today, many nontraditional Jews are migrating back to traditional practices, including being kosher.
And with food being so important in the Jewish home,
I would like to introduce to you this two-pronged program
that marries good health and kosher eating.

"To insure good health: Eat lightly, breathe deeply, live moderately, cultivate cheerfulness, and maintain an interest in life."

— WILLIAM LOUDEN

Luscious and Luxurious: the Other Side of Being Kosher

Over time, I learned that being kosher is absolutely not exclusionary (you certainly don't have to be Jewish to enjoy it!); not only that, it can be an incredibly delicious and deeply holistic way to live because it nourishes your spiritual side through the way you feed and treat your body on the whole. And the icing on my personal napoleons? Being kosher is absolutely ideal if you are trying to live a healthier, weight-conscious lifestyle, and reducing your fat, cholesterol, and salt intake, all while eating marvelous meals. Gone are the days of kosher pizza dripping with grease, of kosher meat or poultry so salty you could barely taste its natural goodness, of your grandmother's pound cake that actually weighed three pounds, of fat-laden halvah or sugary sorbets; enter instead a revolutionary approach to great living, with healthful gourmet kosher meals, including dishes like beef bordeaux, parmesan crème brûlée, and rich soy panna cotta. Today being kosher is one of the easiest and most innate ways of maintaining great health while eating mouthwatering gourmet menus: delectable, naturally low-fat soy products and tofu-based versions of dairy products are easy to find virtually everywhere, high-quality kosher organic meats abound, and flavor-packed salt-free seasonings and egg substitutes are sold across the country in every store, making it very easy to adapt to this extremely healthy diet. Kosher food can be exciting, mouthwateringly delicious, deeply sophisticated, downright urbane, and a natural complement to the kosher jet-setter's way of life; and it's at the very epicenter of my secret recipe!

Kosher Is Accessible!

If you're entertaining the idea of becoming kosher, there has never been an easier time.
The quality, taste, and choices of kosher food are now world-class, and the best news of all?
Fruits, vegetables, and whole grains have always been kosher!

Do I Have to Be Jewish?

When most of us think about "kosher" or "kosher food," we naturally, automatically connect it to Judaism. And it's true: all over the world, many Jewish people of nearly every variety "keep kosher" to some degree, and have done so for a mind-boggling 5,700 years. The good news, though, is that you needn't be Jewish to enjoy a kosher lifestyle; the benefits are so wide-reaching and universal that absolutely everyone can enjoy this spectacularly healthy, delicious way to live, no matter how they practice their spirituality. For me, of course, being kosher weds my spiritual side to my earthbound being, but it can also be an excellent way for anyone to maintain a delicious connection to a lifestyle rich in naturally pure, healthy, safe, and luscious foods. Every day, studies are being done that show us how a kosher lifestyle is not only good for the soul; it may also be scientifically great for the body, aiding in the reduction of cholesterol and fat, and facilitating in digestion. For example, our bodies digest milk products and meat products in very different ways, with the help of different digestive enzymes; if we enjoy kosher meals, those products are never eaten together, making it far easier for us to absorb them and reap their healthy benefits.

Remember:

You don't have to be Jewish to be kosher!
And even if you love to treat yourself
to a breakfast of bacon and whole-grain pancakes every once in a while,
you can still have them and be kosher:
just buy turkey or soy bacon instead of the usual pork-based variety,
and you'll never miss a thing.

LIVING THE ELEGANT KOSHER LIFESTYLE

... is far more than just about what one eats. It's really about the way one lives in one's day-to-day life: it combines respect for how one eats, respect for the maintenance and continuation of a 5,000-year-old tradition, respect for spirituality and holistic health, and finally, respect for the good life and sharing it with the people you love. Kosher foods are exceptionally flavorful as well as profoundly healthy and, yes, sexy, often with culinary roots connecting directly to the magnificent Mediterranean, where people are vigorous, robust, and dedicated to the good life (they've already figured out the Kosher Billionaire's Secret Recipe!).

"The world is round and the place which may seem
like the end may also be only the beginning."

—Ivy Baker

The Sumptuous Kosher Lifestyle on the Road

The Jewish people have been known for more than five millennia as "the wandering people"; we have tended, throughout history, to be migratory, moving from the Middle East and Israel throughout Europe, the western and southern Mediterranean, South America, North America ... even Asia! And I am no different! Sure, I love coming back home, but travel is my passion and my glory, and I have touched down everywhere from Italy to Australia, from France to Japan, and beyond. Like the Jewish people who have come before me, I have taken my kosher lifestyle with me everywhere and made the thrilling discovery that no matter where I eat—whether in the beautifully appointed private home of a celebrity or an inviting château in the south of France, I have always been able to maintain my kosher lifestyle with ease and comfort. And the icing on my triple-layered chocolate cake? I discovered that my healthy kosher lifestyle has been embraced by celebrities and presidents alike. But how is it possible to remain kosher on the road as well as the home? Simple! By following some of the primary components of my Kosher Billionaire's Secret Recipe.

Wherever we live, whether we hail from the West or the Far East, and no matter how we practice reverence toward something, anything, greater than ourselves, certain truths are universal. First, we all respect and value the fruits of the earth, from the food we eat to the wine that many of us take as a sacrament in one form or another. Second, we all need and desire a joyous sustenance of the body, which expresses itself in the way we enjoy physical pursuits and the way we prize corporeal beauty in every form. And finally, most of us like to celebrate the magnificence of other cultures, no matter how alien they may be to us. These three states of pleasure are what separate us, literally, from the animal kingdom around us.

This book is all about the happy marriage of body, mind, and soul. Just as food and drink sustain and fuel our bodies, the pleasure they can bring—especially in the presence of beloved friends and family—are essential to the joy of being alive and give us the opportunity to be thankful for the bounty of the earth.

Secret Recipe

*I love the power of feeling and looking great, of maintaining my inner health
and outer glow through my kosher lifestyle. But how is it possible to remain kosher and healthy, both
on the road and in the air, as well as at home?*

If you're entertaining at home, simply follow my recipes and menus.

*If you're eating in a restaurant, eat either meat (if it is kosher) or dairy, but not both.
Or better still, stick with fish! Request that your meal be cooked with extra virgin olive oil instead of butter.*

*If you're traveling by air, plan to customize your meal order in advance; most airlines will be pleased to help you.
See if they have any kosher wines on board, and if not, ask if you may bring your own.*

*If you're eating a preset menu in someone's home or at a restaurant and one course is not kosher,
simply request that it be replaced by a small pasta course or a salad.*

*Strive to eat the freshest fish available, but not shellfish or other crustaceans, which are "bottom feeders"
and therefore unhealthy.*

Enjoy fresh fruits, vegetables, whole grains, and healthy soy products freely.

*Grab your honey, stretch your legs, and take a stroll after dinner, preferably along the beach under the stars.
Keep that metabolism moving!*

And remember: everyone can live the life of a kosher billionaire!

"When starting the program with Stacy and her husband, my goal was to teach them a healthy lifestyle, not to put them on a restrictive eating plan.
Most people make the mistake of 'going on a diet' rather than making permanent changes in their eating habits.
They may be successful in losing weight temporarily, but most, up to 95 % based on the latest figures, regain the weight, and even more.
With the Cohens, I implemented smaller changes over time, combined with both strength training and aerobic exercise to produce moderate but lasting weight loss.
I wanted them to understand what they were eating, and how and why they were exercising so that even on vacation, at dinner parties, on their private plane,
and on the occasional weekend when their chefs were not cooking for them, they knew what to eat and how to balance out the occasional indulgence."

—Dr. Melina Jampolis

Stacy's Program for Living a Healthy Kosher Life

My goal in writing this book, first and foremost, is to give options to people eating kosher and to share with you my action-packed, glamour-filled life—my secrets, tips, and strategies for living the good life, so that you can see how easy and wonderful it is to feel and look great, how to glow from the inside out, and how those things are solidly connected to a lifestyle that you can enjoy in your own day-to-day lives. My life is filled to the brim with delicious opulence; magnificent kosher foods and spectacular wines are a daily experience for me, and I am extremely grateful for them. Dining with celebrities and traveling the globe is a normal occurrence. Admittedly, though, this enthralling life of decadence once translated into a life filled with too heavy foods on a regular basis, and when my husband and I discovered that it was actually affecting our health—our weight, our blood pressure, our cholesterol, our fat and salt intake—we decided that we had to make a positive change that would allow us to enjoy the delightful kosher foods we love and the dynamic kosher lifestyle we live. We sought out help from Dr. Melina Jampolis, an internationally known nutritionist and host of the Discovery Channel's *The Diet Doctor*. Working together with Dr. Jampolis, we learned that we could keep eating the delicious foods we love so much, lose weight, and strengthen our bodies simultaneously, without ever restricting what we ate or where we traveled.

Miraculously, by adapting Dr. Jampolis's suggestions and then applying them to our lifestyle, I realized I'd hit on another part of the Kosher Billionaire's Secret Recipe: that food, as much as I love it, is actually fuel, that it keeps my metabolism moving, and an active metabolism will usually result in weight loss or at least prevent weight gain. Unlike restrictive diets that exclude this, or cut out that, causing middle-of-the-night (or day!) cravings and weight gain, I realized that by adapting Dr. Jampolis's advice to our kosher lifestyle, and sitting down to eat three meals a day plus two or more healthy snacks, instead of having a nosh here or a bite there while on the run, I was actually eating more, and weighing less!

Stacy's Favorite Healthy Snacks

Edamame
High-protein, low-fat, and utterly delicious, these peel-as-you-eat soybeans are a snacking staple for me.

Hummus
Low in fat and high in flavor, this traditional chickpea puree is also surprising low in calories ... but still very filling!
Enjoy it with whole wheat pita bread or as a dip for, raw vegetables like cucumber, carrots, or bell peppers.

Low-fat yogurt
Smooth, creamy, and packed with calcium, this old standby is a regular in my refrigerator!

"There are two educations.
One should teach us how to make a living and the other how to live."

—John Adams

The Program

What is the program all about? Three things: moderation, balance, and making the right choices! How easy is that? So easy that even a jet-setting kosher James Bond could do it, in between spoonfuls of kosher whitefish caviar and flutes of kosher champagne!

Nourish your body by choosing the right foods.

- *Keep meats lean: choose skinless poultry and leaner cuts of meat.*
- *Make lean protein the focus of your meals: it will keep you from feeling hungry, is more filling than carbohydrates, and has fewer calories than fat.*
- *Choose good fats: eat foods with hearty-healthy oils high in omega-3 fatty acids and mono- and polyunsaturated fats, like extra virgin olive oil, canola oil, avocado, unsalted nuts, flaxseed oil, fatty fish (like salmon).*
- *Cook with only one egg yolk for every six egg whites.*
- *Always choose low-fat dairy products whenever possible.*
- *Season your food with fresh or dried herbs for a punch of flavor, and retrain your palate to reduce your salt.*
- *Choose fresh fruit instead of juices filled with sugar and simple carbohydrates.*
- *Choose complex carbohydrates—whole grains, fresh fruit, fresh vegetables—instead of simple, refined carbohydrates that break down too quickly into sugar (white bread, sugar, white grains).*

Eat a balanced diet.

- *Eating small amounts of everything will result in a happier, healthier metabolism.*
- *Eating regularly, throughout the day, will boost your metabolism, especially if you focus on lean proteins.*
- *Refrain from eating starches at night: starch is fuel, and you need it far less at night when you are the least active.*

Always remember: moderation is everything!

- *If you've eaten a lean meal, splurge on a small dessert; if you've had a larger dessert (and who among us doesn't love a larger dessert?), keep yourself in check the next day and focus on fruits and vegetables in smaller portions.*
- *Instead of sharing that fabulous bottle of vintage kosher bordeaux you and your hubby have been coveting, invest in a wine storage system to keep it fresh for the next night, then share half the bottle, and pop it into the fridge.*

and finally ...

- *Get your body moving!*
- *Go dancing, learn the mambo, take the stairs instead of the elevator, play a round of tennis or golf, go for a walk with the dog, stroll through a museum, go window-shopping, run in the sand, swim in the sea, dig in your garden, play with the baby, take a yoga class ... but just keep moving!*

As it turns out, our need for a healthy kosher lifestyle wound up being nutritionist's dream. Luckily for me—and for you—another key to the Kosher Billionaire's Secret Recipe is worth its weight in Cartier platinum! Eating a healthy kosher diet is anti-allergen, is heart-healthy, eliminates toxins, regulates the circulatory system, includes plenty of fresh fruits and vegetables and neutral complex carbohydrates (which are *pareve*, which means they can be served with either meat or dairy meals), and small but regular amounts of meat, fish, or low-fat dairy. Could there be a healthier, easier, more fabulous way to enjoy life?

Eat, Drink, and Be Merry:

The Kosher Billionaire's Wine Cellar

Over the last twenty years, hundreds of scientific studies have come out pointing to the spectacular health benefits of wine; the world's oldest sacramental drink, wine, it happens, is as great for the heart as it is for the soul! Dr. Jampolis taught me that one to two glasses of wine enjoyed every day may actually lower your risk of heart disease, stroke, and high blood pressure. And in my home, wine is as important to me as the water I drink and the magnificent kosher foods I eat. To enjoy a perfectly matched wine with a sumptuous meal is a heavenly gift; chosen correctly, wine makes food taste better, and food makes wine taste better. Beyond that, it has been proven that wine enjoyed with a kosher meal will actually help digestion. As pleasurable and sensual as luscious kosher food is, so too is wine; we eat and drink with the same senses, so it would be logical that these two major components of our kosher life are interconnected. My husband and I savor the sensual ritual of opening up the perfect vintage kosher burgundy to be enjoyed with an expertly prepared kosher meal, or popping the cork on a luxurious bottle of kosher champagne to drink to the health of our families or our life together.

I tend to entertain with European lavishness; in my opinion, absolutely every meal should be an experience to be relished, and enjoyed to the fullest. When my husband and I have celebrity friends to our home, I have them try to guess the wines we bring up from our wine cellar. Each wine has its own tale to tell, and it invariably does, and provides another facet to the evening as we enjoy the company of our guests. With every swirl of the wine, a new story and a memorable moment are born.

"Nothing more excellent or valuable than the juice of grapes was ever granted by the gods to man."

—PLATO

The Wine Lover's Delight:
a Game of Skill ...

One of my favorite activities to partake with my guests is a game I've named The Wine Lover's Delight. A fabulous way to break the ice, it tests my dinner companions' wine knowledge while introducing them to delicious new vintages and styles of the kosher wines I love to serve with dinner in my home. Before the guests arrive, I lightly tape a small piece of paper over each wine label, making note of what each wine is so that only I am clued in. When everyone arrives, I ask each guest to guess what they're drinking. Sometimes they're right on the billion dollars, and other times they even surprise themselves! But either way, it's a terrific way to learn more about each wine's "nose" and "finish" and results in a heightened awareness of this nectar of the gods.

An Exercise in Pleasure

The enjoyment of wine can be a hugely sensual and deeply fulfilling experience ... if you know how to slow down and savor the moment! Try this sexy little exercise the next time you're at home, waiting for your honey to join you: Shut off the television, send the kids over to their grandmother's, turn off the cell phone, the BlackBerry, and unplug the computer. Now, get dressed: unearth that little Zac Posen number from the depths of your closet and take out two of the finest pieces of stemware you own—perhaps the expensive Baccarat glasses that you reserve for special occasions. If you fancy a fruity white wine, like a Bordeaux, or a Chablis from the Loire Valley, chill it to perfection—immerse it in an ice bath for an hour, or in the fridge for two to bring its temperature down to an ideal 45 to 50 degrees; if you prefer red, maybe a Château Léoville-Poyferré from Bordeaux or an earthy Labet Château de la Tour Clos Vougeot from Burgundy, chilled to 55 degrees. Await your hubby's arrival, open the bottle and let it breathe a bit. Then sit him down, hand him his glass, and tell him how happy you are to have met a kosher billionaire in the making ... even if he's really just the man you love. Savor the nose of the wine; close your eyes, inhale, let it embrace your senses, and take a small taste. Let the sparks fly!

"Wine is proof that God loves us and loves to see us happy."

—Benjamin Franklin

In our home, we tend to prefer classic, elegant French wines rich in *terroir*—the indescribable set of earthy circumstances that marry soil to climate, and vine to fruit—ultimately resulting in each wine's unique properties and tastes.

43

Kosher Wines Around the Globe

Kosher wines are now being produced all over the world, from Chile to Australia, from California to France. So vast is the array, so wide the availability, and so high the quality that there really is no need to drink nonkosher wines anymore if you choose not to. In order to familiarize yourself with what is available, I suggest partaking in another component of my secret recipe: have a regular wine tasting in your home. Tasting four or five wines in moderation (no more than a glass and a half per person, total) is the perfect way to sample new wines that you would not necessarily have tried before. To do this, visit your favorite wine shop, tell the clerk what you have planned, give him the price you'd like to spend on each bottle, and have him make suggestions. He'll be more than happy to help!

Having your Cake and Drinking It Too

Would James Bond ever give up his beloved kosher Grey Goose martinis (shaken, not stirred)? Absolutely not! Is it possible to live a fabulously healthy kosher lifestyle, enjoy magnificent wines the way we do, and still maintain optimal weight and a vigorous glow? The great news is, yes! A vital part of the Kosher Billionaire's Secret Recipe is the understanding that when we drink wine—which we do virtually every night with dinner—we serve the most wonderful wines we can find, and then drink them in absolute moderation. My husband and I will savor half a bottle of a velvety vintage burgundy from a vineyard hundreds of years old, and then we'll close the bottle to be enjoyed on another evening, or we'll simply share a bottle with another couple. Half a bottle of wine equals roughly one and a half glasses each—the perfect amount to enjoy with dinner and to keep empty wine calories to a minimum but reap the benefits that it has to offer.

Drink the most fabulous wines you can find, and drink them often.
Just enjoy them in moderation—no more than a glass and a half with dinner—and you'll keep empty wine
calories to a minimum while taking pleasure in the sensual and healthy benefits they offer.

LIVING THE OPULENT KOSHER LIFESTYLE:
IT'S FOR EVERYONE

As you've seen, it is easy and deliciously fun to step into my Christian Louboutin pumps and travel with me through the kosher world I inhabit every day! Forget exclusionary! Forget heavy! The way I feed my body is nothing short of a red carpet ride through the splendor that brings together high-quality, gourmet fare, spirituality, sumptuous wines, and memorable experiences, all adding up to inner health and outer glow. So take my hand and together we'll travel through this opulent world so that you too can make it your own and live the life of a kosher billionaire!

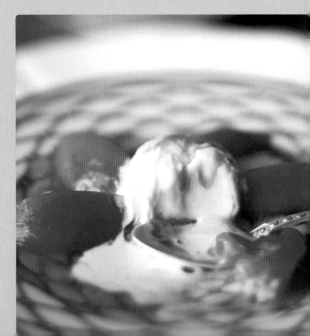

A Nobel Prize-Winning Menu

Appetizer
Tuna Tartar with Broccolini Salad and Pickled Red Onion
Baron Herzog Sauvignon Blanc 2003, Central Coast, California

Entrée
Beef Bordeaux with Creamy Saffron-Potato Puree
Château Léoville-Poyferré Saint Julien 2001, Bordeaux, France
or
Seitan Braised in Red Wine with Thyme and Onions
Teal Lake Petit Verdot Cabernet 2002, Southeastern Australia

Salad
White and Green Asparagus Salad with Citrus Lavender Vinaigrette

Dessert
Apricot Agrodolce with Vanilla Soy Ice Cream
Chainier Clos de Nouys Vouvray Moelleux 2002, Loire Valley, France

The Kosher Billionaire's Secret Inspiration

Aperitif
Laurent-Perrier Brut nv Champagne, France

Appetizer
Moroccan-Style Chickpea and Vegetable Terrine
Verbau Gewürztraminer 2001, Alsace, France

Entrée
Grilled Marinated Salmon with Beet Carpaccio
Domaine Pierre Labet Beaune-Coucherias 1er Cru 2004, Burgundy, France

Salad
Winter Porcini Salad

Dessert
Stacy's Kiss: Soy Panna Cotta
Bartenura Limone Liqueur, Italy

When my guests hear about our healthy kosher lifestyle,
they are thrilled to know that they are also dining so deliciously on a nutritionally sound program!
Just serve a healthy kosher meal, and savor the compliments that you'll surely receive!

LIVING THE GOOD LIFE

"If you wish to live with civility,
it is always important to aim to please your guest."

—STACY COHEN

Chapter II

The Kosher Billionaire's Secret Recipe for Entertaining

The opulent table is set before you with crystal Baccarat goblets waiting to be filled with extraordinary vintage wines; sprays of fresh-cut Casablanca lilies and rare peonies adorn each magnificent place setting; candlelight bathes the room with a warm, dusky glow that casts a certain mystique on all who enter; you greet each guest as they arrive with an iced glass of nearly frozen sake, putting a modern twist on the ages-old tradition of welcoming visitors with a cocktail. Tonight you will treat them to a dinner served with luxury, grace, and health; together you will enjoy a sumptuous healthy kosher meal, created and presented with elegance and the assurance that your guests will leave your home with memories of generous extravagance vivid enough to last a lifetime.

Entertaining and living this way is not just for billionaires; it's for everyone, and I want to share with you the ways in which you too can experience the wondrous joy of being an elegant host or hostess to the people you entertain.

The Kosher Billionaire's Secret Recipe will teach you how to reach for the stars, create spectacular kosher meals and menus, and entertain with finesse and elegance, all while focusing on great health! This is all simply a part of the secret recipe to living the good life, whoever you are, and wherever you live. In fact, I've learned that indulging your guests is as much a gift to yourself and to your spirit as it is to them!

There's nothing I love more than entertaining—from setting the scene with beautiful linens, sparkling glassware, fresh flowers, and warm lighting to dressing for the occasion and the excitement of the guests arriving. Most of all, I love opening my home to laughter and love and sharing. That's what entertaining is all about, and I always get back so much more than I give.

My grandmother was the quintessential hostess, and it was from her that I learned how to be attentive to my guests' needs, keeping their glasses full, checking on special food requests, and always, above all else, making them feel comfortable. Today, when entertaining, I always ask my guests in advance if they have any special dietary needs, so that I can be as accommodating as possible, and then indulge them with their preferences.

I always make sure to have exciting entertainment on hand that sets the tone and theme for the evening, be it a fun magic act to break the ice, mariachi singers to get everyone in a jovial mood, Hawaiian dancers for a sultry tropical edge, or Italian opera for pure romance. I want our guests to feel as if our estate, which we call "the love house," is *their* home; we open our doors and our guests join us in a warm environment replete with welcoming accoutrements, from a lovely fire in the fireplace, if there's a chill in the air, to candles, to the finest red wine imaginable.

Today, when I entertain, I always ask my guests if they have any special dietary needs,
so that we can be as accommodating as possible, and then indulge them with their preferences.

Abraham had a tent in the middle of the desert, and was the greatest host to everyone who passed by his desert home. One day some angels came through his oasis, and he washed their feet and gave them food and drink. At the same time, God wanted to talk to him, but Abraham said, "God, can you wait? I'm entertaining guests." This was shocking! How was it possible that he would ask God to wait? But God said, "Okay, I'll wait." For God, the biggest *mitzvah*, or blessing, is hospitality and treating other people in your home the way you treat yourself, and letting people feel as if your home is their home and making them feel wonderful. Abraham was the world's first hospitable entrepreneur, who created the land that can be sowed, planted, harvested, and resowed, thus providing the world with much of the food we eat and the wine we drink.

"There are no days in life so memorable as those which
vibrated to some stroke of the imagination."

—RALPH WALDO EMERSON

MAKING EVERY MEAL SPECIAL, THE KOSHER BILLIONAIRE WAY

When I cook privately for friends, I always strive to make every meal a gracious, special celebration.
I keep an "entertaining diary," where I jot down important details like special seating arrangements
I've designed to bring people together and inspire them to meet each other;
I make note of their special eating requirements, favorite dishes, and, naturally, their favorite wines or champagne,
right down to the dress I'll be wearing on the occasion!
When I entertain guests who have different kinds of dietary needs, I also always find it helpful
to prepare several smaller dishes that function like "tapas" (in Spain) and "mezze" (in Greece).
Be as creative as you want, but always be as healthful and as gracious as you can!

Having expensive china is not a requirement for the secret recipe, but having fun with your meals is an absolute necessity! So whether you're serving yourself and your sweetheart, or you're having an elegant dinner party, don't ever be afraid to use playful colors that make you feel enlightened, and that you can automatically associate with a dairy or meat meal.

If you want to serve a meal that's fit for King David, do away with the place mats and the tablecloths, and let the magnificent grain of your wooden dining room table shine through; set your china, silverware, plates, and candelabra directly on it, and your meal will be a royal stunner!

The Opulent Kosher Kitchen

The secret recipe for sumptuous and elegant entertaining really begins in the kitchen; that is the room where a celebration—or even just a quietly romantic dinner between the two of you—starts, with the planning of creative menus, the preparation of magnificent dishes, and their presentation for serving. As we've seen, being kosher is an eons-old tradition that necessitates keeping meat and dairy dishes apart; even different utensils are used for the different meals. This enables me to nurture my spiritual side, even as I'm entertaining the people I love.

In my home, it gives me a sense of well-being to keep thousands of years of tradition alive by following the laws of *kashrut* (the Hebrew word for "keeping kosher"). In keeping with these principles, I use different sets of cookware and utensils for meals that are meat-based and those that are dairy-based. This also gives me the opportunity to spread my creative entertaining wings and serve different types of meals on different-colored plates; for example, I serve dairy meals on my Fabergé plates that have a beautiful, peaceful motif around the rim, and meat-based meals on Christofle plates featuring a whimsical center design ringed by different rim colors. This way, separating meat and dairy can be as easy to remember as it is beautiful! And remember, anything that is *pareve* is considered "neutral" and can be served with meat or dairy!

But having fine china is not essential to entertaining; it's how you display what you serve. What is most important when entertaining is that you make your guests feel welcome, that the food you serve is elegant, delicious, and beautiful, and that you pay attention to the smallest detail: every facet counts ... just like a diamond!

*The simple elegance
added by a flower laid at every place setting is unbeatable ...*

The Fine Art of Entertaining

Entertaining is a joy and a pleasure, and a wonderful way for the kosher billionaire inside you to show how much your friends, family, and loved ones mean to you. And while the food you serve is very important, the manner in which you serve it, the slow and special way in which you serve wine—with all the royal majesty it deserves—and the way you make your guests feel when they walk into your home are of paramount importance. Ambience plays a big role in the way your guests will feel as they enter your home, and even the most simply and humbly decorated home can be made romantic, warm, welcome, and luxurious with thoughtful touches. I believe that the atmosphere of a home depends on the very special, personal way in which its owners have set the actual mood and feeling of the home. Is it warm and welcoming? Romantic and inviting? Eclectic, relaxed, and slightly funky? Odds are that your guests' experience when you entertain them will reflect the mood you've created in your home.

In my home, I love to transform our rooms with the simple elegance of candlelight: there is something indescribable about the softness of the glow that can quickly and easily take any space from lovely to gorgeous. Throughout history, photographers, film directors, and even painters have understood the magical radiance cast by candlelight; warm and deeply inviting, it provides an almost magnetic pull to everything it touches. Placed strategically—near glass or mirrors, for example, where the light not only diffuses into the space but actually reflects off the surfaces around it—candles provide timeless elegance and make any space stunning. These glowing additions are simple to achieve, and can be as basic as adding two candles to a lavishly appointed dinner table set with beautiful china and stemware, to strategically placing twelve or fourteen pillar candles throughout a room. Another simple way to make any room more inviting, warm, and romantic is the addition of flowers, which provide not only color and texture, but the sense that one is bringing the outside in, with all its natural glory; just make sure that the flowers for the room in which you're serving are less aromatic than those that you bring into a room designed for after-dinner conversation (the library, den, or deck, which I consider an outdoor room). This way, the fragrance of the flowers will not compete with the mouthwatering aromas coming from the kitchen and the perfume coming from the wineglasses! Again, every detail counts, so it's okay to splurge (within your budget!) on these feasts for the eye. And don't stop at vases: the simple elegance of a flower laid at every place setting is unbeatable.

A primary component of the Kosher Billionaire's Secret Recipe is the understanding that every meal can be an utterly delightful celebration—of your friends, your family, yourselves—and be wonderfully healthy at the same time. No matter how plentiful or relaxed your healthy kosher meals are, always strive to entertain with elegance fun, whimsy, and all the luxury that a kosher billionaire deserves!

PAMPERING YOUR GUESTS, ADDING ROMANCE

"When you give, you find you will receive much more."

—STACY COHEN

There is a certain incomparable joy that I get when I know my guests are happy and contented, and it goes far beyond the delicious healthy kosher meals and fine wines I serve when I entertain them. Taking care of my guests is not only a gift to them, though: it is a gift to me, because I know I've made my family and friends feel special in our home. Candles can certainly provide romantic allure to a room of any style, but again, so can flowers, the addition of a fireplace in the dining room (I actually added mine!), making the perfect wine selections to complement the meal you'll prepare, the right music (I like to play soft jazz, classical, rhythm and blues, or opera), even the smallest detail, like an expertly folded napkin, can make your already delicious menu taste even more spectacular!

How to Make Every Healthy Kosher Meal a Special Occasion

Make sure to learn about your guests' dietary needs before planning the meal, and go all-out to accommodate them.
Welcome your guests to your home with something unexpected when they arrive: an icy glass of sake, a stem or two
of their very favorite flower, a printed copy of the menu for the evening.
Or, for a new twist on the printed menu, include which wines you will be serving
and a story or history of the wines. It is a great conversation piece.
At the end of the evening, send your guests home with a special bottle of wine, a rare bottle of olive oil, or, if you
have a garden, some beautiful cut flowers. It creates stunning and lasting memories, and illustrates love of giving.
Select music that matches the mood of the celebration:
Jazz: Elegant, timeless, intoxicatingly sultry. Blues: fun, laid-back, relaxed.
Classical: Traditional, formal, chic. Opera: Highly romantic, ethereal, serene.
Consider bringing in an entertainer to perform jazz or even opera,
and make your living room your own personal Lincoln Center!
Choose stunning varieties of flowers that give off little or no fragrance, like calla lilies or unscented peonies,
so that they don't compete with the luscious aroma of the healthy kosher dishes and wines you're serving.
Place clusters of fragrance-free candles around the room as well as on the dining room table,
for maximum romantic ambience.

When serving wine, pour no more than three ounces into each glass;
the wine will breathe more fully and open up like the petals of a flower. Ask your guests to swirl this nectar,
take in its smell and bouquet, hold it to the light and see its true color, and then, finally, savor it slowly.
Wine is not water; it's meant to be sipped slowly and enjoyed thoroughly.

The Kosher Billionaire's Romantic Dinner for Two

This delightfully romantic, flavor-packed, multicourse meal is specifically designed to slow you down and ask you to experience every bite. By starting off with an aperitif or a glass of champagne, your palate will be cleansed and ready for the mélange of flavors that follows. The dishes themselves are light, the colors magnificent, and the sensational tastes, worthy of a kosher billionaire!

Your dinner will be even more romantic when you look into each other's eyes as you toast to your love ...

Menu

Aperitif
Champagne or an aperitif wine
Laurent-Perrier Cuvée Rosé Brut nv Champagne, France

Appetizer
Orzotto with Asparagus
Weinstock Cellar Select Sauvignon Blanc 2005, Central Coast, California

Entrée
Pan-Seared Ahi Tuna Scottato with Red Onion Marmalade and Herb Salad
Bodegas Ramon Bilbao Rioja Crianza 2003, Rioja, Spain

Dessert
Roasted Figs with Fromage Blanc and Red Wine Sauce
Bartenura Malvasia 2005, Salento IGT, Italy

FIRESIDE DINNER PARTY

When the weather begins to turn chilly, I love to move the party a bit closer to our dining-room fireplace and serve menus that warm the body as well as the soul. But don't let the weather dictate your entertaining mood: even if it's sweltering outside, simply lower the thermostat a bit, build that roaring fire, and pretend that baby, it's cold outside!

As with all my secret recipes, this resplendent meal is light but packed with flavor to warm you no matter what the weather.

Menu

Appetizer
Beef Carpaccio with Fresh Figs and Shaved Vegetable Salad
Bartenura Valpolicella 2003, Veneto, Italy

Entrée
Spicy Chicken Paprikash with Vegetable Tagliatelle and Celery Root Puree
Domaine Pierre Labet Beaune-Coucherias 1er Cru 2004, Burgundy, France

Salad
Herbed Couscous with Feta and Orange

Dessert
Apple Granita with Yogurt and Granola
Château Piada, Sauternes 2001, Bordeaux, France

LET'S TRAVEL
TOGETHER

"Let your faith show you the way."

—STACY COHEN

Is there a way to pamper yourself when you travel and yet maintain your new, healthy kosher lifestyle, no matter your means?
There is, if you know how to be innovative, and reach for the stars!

CHAPTER III

THE KOSHER BILLIONAIRE'S SECRET RECIPE
FOR LIVING THE GREAT LIFE IN THE AIR AND ON THE ROAD

On a spectacular cloudless day, you stroll out onto the velvet-smooth jetway. A sleek plane awaits you, the thrum of its engine purring as it prepares to whisk you away. After a graceful, birdlike takeoff, you're airborne, winging through the sky at nearly the speed of sound. Floating serenely 43,000 feet above the earth, you leave behind the cares of your daily life; wrapped in a luxurious three-ply, sky-blue cashmere shawl you treated yourself to while shopping at that little boutique on the Avenue Montaigne, your thoughts now turn to the verdant hills of Tuscany. You dream of Florence, and of your old-money friends with the Tuscan villa nestled in the hills above Greve; you imagine a delightful alfresco lunch of freshly grilled, lemon-infused dorado at that funky little boutique hotel in Viareggio, the sun-drenched Italian Riviera sprawled before you. You yearn for that magnificently romantic Hawaiian sunset dinner you shared with your husband, while paparazzi—thinking that your handsome hunk was James Bond and you were one of the Bond girls—followed you in a chopper; you dream of that ritzy château in St. Moritz, where you napped contentedly after a day of serious skiing and even more serious shopping at some of the most plush shops in the world, before enjoying a deliciously healthy kosher multicourse meal at a St. Moritz hotspot. Are these travel dreams fit for Ari Onassis … or a kosher billionaire? Yes—both! And you, too!

Gone are the days when luxurious travel meant ten days on an ocean liner, five Louis Vuitton steamer trunks packed with every item you owned, and stiff, stodgy food salted to inedibility (to preserve its freshness for the long journey) and served 'round the clock.

71

These days, travel is purposely speedy, designed simply to get you where you need to be quickly, so that you can enjoy your destination rather than the actual getting there. From electronic check-in counters to no-frills airlines offering little service, often horrible "food" and seats designed for a pint-sized twelve-year-old, the ages-old fine art of travel has been reduced to virtually nothing. But is there a happy medium between tedious travel (where you were so overfed and exhausted by the time you arrived that you were too depleted to do anything but turn around and come home) and the modern-day equivalent of an airborne fast food restaurant (where the food is terrible, the service worse, but you're in and out in a hurry)? Is there a way to make travel an exciting treat and maintain your new, healthy kosher lifestyle no matter your means? There is, if you know how to reach for the stars! Enter the Kosher Billionaire's Secret Recipe for lofty travel! Remember, style and creativity, comfort and ease are limited only by your imagination.

Be Prepared!

If the prospect of a less-than-perfect in-flight meal concerns you,
make sure you let the airline know ahead of time exactly what your needs are, and ask them to customize
a meal for you. They'll do all they can to give you exactly what you need. Food courts and airplane food
can be the enemy, and hotel minibars don't help either. How to deal with this unhealthy food onslaught?
Be prepared!
I often call ahead to the hotel where I'm staying and ask the staff to please remove
the snacks from the minibar, and replace those chocolate bars with trays of fresh vegetables
from room service. Add a yogurt dip or some hummus, and you're healthy, kosher, and guilt-free!

No matter where I travel, when my celebrity friends have flown on my private aircraft, they too have had the chance to dine on the delicious cuisine that we enjoy every day, and they are always astonished at how delicious it is ... including Jennifer Lopez. During Fashion Week 2006, Jennifer flew to New York to attend a spectacular Scottish-inflected event thrown by fashion "bad boy" Alexander McQueen at the Metropolitan Museum of Art. At what was the most exclusive affair of the week, I was thrilled to be a special guest of Donatella Versace, along with Jennifer (who lightened everything up by telling us how tight her gown was), her husband, singer Marc Anthony, and superstar Lenny Kravitz (who sat next to me!). The night was star-studded with mysterious and elegant celebrities, including the handsome and dapper Rupert Everett, dressed in Scottish finery; Linda Evangelista, resplendent in Yves Saint Laurent; Charlize Theron, in Dior by John Galliano (who also designed my wedding dress; it was such a delight to see him again); the charming Elizabeth Hurley; and Donald Trump. On this magical night, young children performed ballet for us, and before long the party was over, and so was this fairy tale evening.

Traveling Like a Kosher Billionaire

Would you like to spend a week in New York, the city that never sleeps, then board a plane, doze off after a deliciously healthy kosher airborne lunch, and wake up in the Caribbean? I do it—frequently—but still, I do not take for granted the super-performance Gulfstream that I travel on: it is the pinnacle of luxury, and it should be treated accordingly. Even at night, the plane looks beautiful, its cavernous cockpit glittering with lights that radiate out onto the tarmac. Once aloft, you can feel how powerful the jet really is, as you gaze out the oversized, round windows at the sunset and catch a glimpse of the signature Gulfstream upturned wing tips parting the skies. Realizing how lucky I am to be able to travel this way forces me to slow down and concentrate on the small details that make travel so exciting. How many of us remember going to the airport as children and watching with a rush of excitement, as the people around us left for far-off lands that we had only read about in myths?

SMALL TOUCHES FOR LUXURIOUS TRAVEL

On a recent trip to an island paradise, my flight attendant greeted me with a compliment, a smile, and a yellow rose that just happened to match the dazzling Versace dress I was wearing. Put immediately at ease by the smallest of special, friendly touches, my flight was relaxed and peaceful, and I was able to focus on the joy of the travel experience and the magnificent tropical wonderland that would be awaiting my arrival on the other end. There are many small ways in which you can make your travel experience opulent enough for a kosher billionaire ... even if your airline is less than lavish:

Luxurious but comfortable travel clothes: Go ahead—be that fabulous traveling fashionista you see in the pages of Vogue! Wear comfortable clothes made of luxe materials: a silk blouse in shimmering colors and doe-soft pull-on lounging trousers made of cashmere will keep you cool in the summer and warm in the colder months, and will take you from the plane to the lobby of the Ritz in kosher billionaire style. Break out those Gucci sunglasses and tie an Hermès scarf onto the handle of your bag to complete the outfit.

Always be prepared to look—and feel—like a billion bucks: You never know who you're going to meet on that next flight: it could be the love of your life, or the business partner of your dreams!

Pack a silk eyeshade in your carry-on: Opt for something really decadent in a slightly funky, brightly colored weave, or a more traditional British paisley, but make sure to take this must-have travel accessory along. You'll block out glare, doze more comfortably, and look like a billion bucks!

Remember your blanket: Forget about those nasty, scratchy blankets that every airline hands out on longer flights. Instead, invest in a sizable pashmina or cashmere shawl that can go the distance with you—as your blanket in the air, as a gorgeous wrap to toss around your shoulders when you land, as a sexy sarong when you go out dancing.

Pack your healthy kosher snacks in style: Don't assume that the kosher menu offered by the airline is edible; it's very likely laden with salt and fat. Most airlines are happy to accommodate a simple request for a plate of fresh fruit and cheese, but if you're not sure what you'll get, travel like a kosher billionaire instead! Pack your own healthy kosher snacks in a high-end fabric tote outfitted with a small freezer pack, and create a lavish picnic in the air; ask the airline ahead of time for clearance to bring your own half bottle of kosher champagne or your favorite kosher wine, and live it up, kosher billionaire style! Perfect packable healthy kosher in-flight snacks include:

- *Fresh vegetables: bell peppers, pea pods, baby carrots.*
- *Hummus with lemon and a dash of paprika.*
- *Heart-healthy unsalted nuts: almonds, peanuts, and pistachios are delicious, filled with the good fats your heart needs, and guaranteed to keep you sated until you reach your destination.*
- *Whole wheat pita.*
- *A petite wedge of a luxuriously delicious semi-hard cheese that will travel well: aged Gouda, Pecorino di Pienza, Toma Piemontese, or heart-healthy herbed soy cheeses are just a few delectable possibilities.*
- *Membrillo, the delectable Spanish guava paste that's filled with fruity flavor, is low in fat and calories, and is a perfect accompaniment to cheese, fresh vegetables, and nuts.*
- *A small square or two of the most decadent chocolate you can find.*
- *A split, or half bottle of chilled kosher champagne, such as vintage Laurent-Perrier, or a chilled half bottle of a delicious vintage kosher white wine.*

Though my jet is opulent, special touches make my journeys even more pleasurable. I personalized the plane by decorating it in my favorite peaceful colors that would soothe and inspire me on my flights; the chairs are made of a soft, neutral leather, the tables are a light cherry wood. I also take special care to plan my in-flight meals well in advance so that I can be sure to maintain my healthy lifestyle even when I'm 43,000 feet in the air.

SHORT FLIGHT OR LONG JOURNEY?

If your flight is going to be shorter than two hours, odds are the meal you'll be served won't, in fact, be a full meal: it will probably just be a snack. But if your flight is going to be longer than three hours—or overnight—you can be assured that you'll be served at least one full meal, depending on the length of the trip and the airline. At the time you make your flight reservations, make sure to specifically discuss your options and ask the airline to customize your healthy kosher meal. The key to maintaining your kosher healthy lifestyle while traveling is to ask questions and avoid surprises!

Not every kosher billionaire can go so far as personalizing the tail of her aircraft the way I did, or outfitting the plane with a bouquet of her favorite roses, so start simple and travel with your own monogrammed napkins, splurge on the latest bestseller, carry your own earphones so that you're able to listen to the movie or to some music in sublime comfort, and dream of your destination!

"Toss your dreams into the air and make a wish:
you might be surprised at what comes back to you ... a new love, a new home, a new you!"

—Stacy Cohen

The Kosher Billionaire's Secret Recipe, on the Road

It's often been said that "getting there is half the fun," and when you travel like a kosher billionaire, it's more than half the fun. By treating yourself well and endeavoring to live the life of a kosher billionaire, you'll discover that you don't have to be Bill Gates or Richard Branson to live (or travel) like them!

But with well-appointed, elegant world travel also comes the delicious temptation of new foods to try, many of which will be alluringly flavor- and fat-filled and perhaps, besides not being kosher, totally unrecognizable to you, your palate, and your waistline. So how do you take up the promise of the Kosher Billionaire's Secret Recipe when you're abroad, visiting all of those miraculous places you've only dreamed about, only to discover that the culinary options may be delicious and abundant ... but off-limits to you? Simple: by following the basic regimen of the Kosher Billionaire's Secret Recipe, you can travel anywhere, eat everywhere, maintain great health, and look terrific, all while fulfilling yourself spiritually and treating your body like the temple that it is.

Playing the Temptation Game

Life is all about having fun ... in moderation!
So go ahead, have a bit more of that decadently rich triple crème Camembert, or that petit gateau.
If your clothes start to feel like they're getting tight, simply slow down a bit,
take an extra yoga class, or work out a little bit more.
Temptation is everywhere: it lurks around every corner where you live
(think about all of those fabulous gourmet ice cream and gelato parlors cropping up,
or even average supermarkets, with their shelves of cookies and cakes), and every corner you visit.
Every country you go to and each culture you immerse yourself in has its own intrinsically delicious ways
of tempting you gastronomically and leading you astray.
But as different as cultures may be, they are all miraculously alike in that each one grows fruits
and vegetables, harvests and mills whole grains, and enjoys fish, meat, or soy for protein.
And these are the food groups that you need to maintain a healthy kosher lifestyle wherever you are.
So whether you're visiting India or Italy, Greece or Japan, don't feel confined
by your healthy kosher lifestyle: embrace it! Rejoice that your healthy program is so universal
that you can comfortably eat from menus around the world, wherever you go.

As different as cultures may be, each one grows fruits and vegetables, harvests and mills whole grains, and enjoys fish, meat, or soy for protein – exactly the food groups you need for a healthy kosher lifestyle wherever you are.

Cook with Flavor

Instead of cooking with salt, try adding a little bit of spice to your food.
Studies have shown that foods rich in spices like garlic, ginger, cumin, and curry are extremely heart-healthy,
may lower blood pressure, and are packed with so much flavor that you'll never, ever miss salt!
And remember, spices don't always have to be hot to be powerful: generally, a little goes a long way.
So chop up some fresh, peeled ginger and add it to a healthy low-fat soy dish, or rub that salmon fillet
with a bit of mild curry, and you'll be amazed at the difference it will make.

The first time I traveled after my healthy lifestyle began, I became hungry,
and I experienced the guilt of breaking my healthy kosher eating plan.
Now, I always plan a snack in advance. This way, I feel happy about what we are eating.

The Joys of Travel Abroad

Travel is one of my dearest and sweetest passions. I have experienced the paradise that is Italy's Amalfi coast and the magnificence that is Israel; I've visited India and Japan; swum in the crystalline waters off the coast of Australia; lived la dolce vita in Paris; marveled at the Prado in Spain; sailed into a mile-deep caldera off Santorini; and relaxed in California to dine at Thomas Keller's restaurant, The French Laundry, in Napa. Wherever I have traveled, I have always been able to maintain my secret recipe lifestyle, to eat healthfully and well, with an eye to my waistline as well as my spirit, always with profound respect for where I am and the people who are serving or dining together with me.

From one side of the globe to the other, my adventures and journeys led me to some remarkable places and introduced me to incredible people.

In Australia, on a visit to the magnificent Sydney Opera House—that stunning, acoustically perfect structure suspended above Sydney Harbor—I felt as if I was walking on water as a luxurious speedboat shuttled me to the breathtaking building to enjoy a concert. Set against a moonlit sky studded by shooting stars, it was the kind of place that inspired all my dreams to come true. Of course, I made a wish or two!

And when it came to the cuisine I enjoyed there, maintaining the Kosher Billionaire's Secret Recipe was an adventure in deliciously fresh, local eating: the culture is so diverse in Australia that southeast Asian, Greek, and Italian culinary influences are extremely common there, and because of the country's proximity to water and its tendency toward extremely healthful and active living, it is virtually impossible not to eat healthfully while you're down under. Fresh produce is regularly available, and the culinary trend is toward low-salt, low-fat cookery incorporating lean meat and lightly cooked, colorful, steamed, or stir-fried vegetables, making it very easy to maintain the Kosher Billionaire's Secret Recipe. The freshest seafood is always just a catch away, and potent Asian flavors like ginger, lemongrass, coriander, and chili crop up in the most unusual places.

Coupling the vibe of Miami with the relaxing atmosphere of Sardinia, Australia was a spectacular getaway that enabled me to easily maintain my healthy kosher lifestyle and indulge my love of the outdoors and magnificent fresh foods. The world's oldest continent, inhabited for more than 60,000 years by Aborigines and settled by the British as a colony more than 200 years ago, displays stunning diversity in every realm—animal, mineral, vegetable, and geological: from the dry outback to the high plateaus of the Great Dividing Range and the verdant woods of Tasmania, Australia is nothing less than a visual sensory explosion, a mind-bogglingly delicious, sun-dappled lifestyle for the people who live there. Australia is also becoming world renowned for wines and entertainment; not only are the vintages from the island of Tasmania extremely popular, so are the casinos!

I was inspired and deeply moved by the vital, rugged beauty that Australia has to offer—from the outback, where I witnessed a kangaroo leaping past us as we drove through the terrain, and a koala perched in a tree with a baby on its back, enjoying a leafy lunch, to the beautiful Gold Coast (which feels like Miami in the 1950s), where I took a few surfing lessons. I was also easily able to apply the Kosher Billionaire's Secret Recipe to my time there. Perhaps, if you're lucky enough, you'll hold court with hunky tennis ace Patrick Rafter!

The Kosher Billionaire's Moveable Feast: Bringing It Home

Travel is my passion and my pleasure; for me, there is nothing quite as stirring or spiritually inspiring as experiencing new cultures, enjoying the spectacular array of delectably healthy foods available everywhere I go, and adapting them to my healthy kosher program. And you can do it too! If you're ever faced with a surfeit of unknown foods that don't quite look familiar to you, or you simply aren't sure about them, never be afraid to ask for what's fresh. Every nation on earth serves delicious vegetables, and everywhere you turn, wonderfully healthy soy-based foods, fish, salads, and pasta are in spectacular abundance. One of the most exciting and delicious things to bring home as that souvenir you'll remember forever is the memory of a spectacular healthy kosher meal you had somewhere romantic and thrilling, like, for example, Italy, Paris, or perhaps Rio de Janeiro.

"Never allow yourself to sit on the sidelines;
get in the game of life!
You have to play to win, but always have a timely exit strategy."

—STACY COHEN

In Brazil, the best way to watch your waistline is to get involved in the waist-slimming dancing at Carnaval.
If you keep your hips moving to the gyrating rhythms, you will need a bodyguard just to keep watch over your beautiful body!

Flying into Rio de Janeiro, with the wheels of the jet nearly touching the hands of the Corcovado, awakens the senses, and gets the blood to circulate faster. Imagine: as your plane touches the ground, the windows of the jet actually steam up from the sultry, tropical environment you're about to enter, and when the doors open, the spice-laden fragrance of Carnaval in the warm February air makes you feel as if you're invincible.

The passion of the Brazilian people makes dancing until dawn and learning how to samba as though you were born to it simply a must. The biggest festival in the world, Carnaval results in evening after evening of Brazilians dressed in brilliantly hued, hip-hugging costumes fashioned from glittery sequins glued directly to the body; dissipating in sweat as the celebrants dance all night into the wee hours of the morning, the sequins leave only faint traces of glitter on their heated bodies as the sun begins to rise, and the celebration starts all over again. The Brazilian passion for Carnaval, and for fabulous street food is outweighed only by the love for futebol—or what we call soccer—which local children, often from the slums, play with bare feet on the hot Rio sand, sometimes using rolled-up newspapers for balls.

An inflamed passion and desire, instilled from a young age, to leave the slums of Rio and become a famous futebol player has made it easy for Brazil to develop one of the finest teams in the world; often they would rather play than eat or drink; instead, they drink in the sport as if it were a sensuous delicacy.

Adapted to your healthy kosher lifestyle, spectacularly delicious international recipes can become part of your daily Kosher Billionaire Secret Recipe, whether you're cooking just for yourself and your beloved, or for a celebration. International recipes can be as precious and valuable as the most expensive souvenir bought on the Champs-Élysées … and a lot more healthy! In my home, I take great pleasure in enjoying mouthwatering healthy kosher adaptations of meals I had in places like Italy and Paris, where food means love, and is as much a part of the culture as the landscape of Provence or Tuscany.

Italy is all about sensual pleasure, from the stunning models strutting their stuff on the runways of Milan to Rome's nearly religious love of their beloved afternoon espresso; from sexy red Lamborghinis that cruise fearlessly on the Autostrada at over 100 miles per hour, to Michelangelo's ripplingly muscular *David* in Florence, to the lust that every Italian feels toward his wine and his cuisine. Even Aldo, our driver in Positano who so assuredly navigated the winding cliffside roads above the Riviera, greeted me every time he saw me with a robust *Buongiorno, bellissima!* Italy is a place that thrives on passion ... so when in Rome ...

THE KOSHER BILLIONAIRE'S SECRET RECIPE CHALLENGE

Although I love to travel the globe and experience absolutely as much as I can, there is no city in the world that speaks of love and la dolce vita as Paris does. From the winding streets of the Left Bank to the broad, tree-lined avenues near Boulevard Haussmann, one can never tire of this magnificent city where beautiful people are everywhere, haute couture is in the air, and the culinary passions have been immortalized through the centuries by legendary superstars, from one of the world's first celebrity chefs, Antonin Carême, to Louis Diat and countless others. It is from the magical City of Light that classical dishes come—braises, roasts, sautés, and, of course, pastries that have been copied all over the world. And why? Because, quite simply, they are the flower of civilization.

Arrive in Paris at your château, and go for a stroll down the alleyways and shaded avenues. Window-shop at the most lavish of boutiques, and take in the brightly colored pastries in the window of the celebrated food shop Fauchon. Pop into the city's many bookstores, tuck a baguette under your arm (even if you intend to eat only a quarter of it!), buy yourself a silk scarf, don your sunglasses, and pretend—if even for a short time—that you're a native Parisian, that this city is yours for the taking, that romance is everywhere, and that you are home. And remember that wherever you go and whatever you eat, you can adapt that luscious dish to your healthy kosher lifestyle. It's as easy as saying *Mais oui!*

You can make memorable romantic moments even when you're by yourself.
Window-shopping and dreaming can be just as pleasurable as actually shopping
... dreams inspire us to create success .

As I walk slowly around the Place Vendôme, the crisp autumn air chills my face. I raise the hood of my leopard-print jacket and, glancing at the large monument commemorating Napoleon's adventures, I think to myself, "He must have had a huge Oedipal complex."

I turn my head to catch my reflection in the window of the glamorous jewelry store Boucheron. Through my dark oval sunglasses, I feel as though I'm Audrey Hepburn in a scene from Breakfast at Tiffany's. Meanwhile, my love has asked for some time alone. Little do I know he is looking for that certain special something for our engagement. After strolling around the square, I step into the Paris Ritz and wait for him in the garden, where Hemingway and countless royalty and painters have relaxed for years. My sweetheart joins me, and together we are whisked off to the Eiffel Tower, where the lights are calling to me like beckoning diamonds. The elevator rises on a slant, the door opens, and I offer my jacket to the coat check clerk, revealing my cream and black lace appliqué Yves Saint Laurent gown. As my husband-to-be and I gaze amorously into each other's eyes moments after being seated, a stranger approaches and offers to take a picture for us. We smile, say yes, and pose … only to notice that the photographer is New York's hero, former mayor Rudy Giuliani!

France isn't all about cities, boulevards, and sidewalks; it always seems like the sun is forever setting as you land in Nice, and drive through sun-drenched Provence, where the olive-, tomato-, and garlic-laden dishes are packed with herbal freshness, cream-based sauces are nonexistent, and dining is a far more relaxed affair, usually done alfresco, or on a covered patio, the height of casual but still extravagant living. Provençal wines are often served in stemless everyday water glasses, meals are cooked over an outdoor fire, and the residents' connection to the earth is palpable everywhere you go.

Not far from Provence lies the independent Principality of Monaco, where I feel most at home. Driving the scenic Moyenne Corniche coastal highway in a 1957 platinum Rolls-Royce, I arrive at the opulent Hôtel de Paris. Packed with history, Monaco has attracted the fashionable set, distinguished royalty, writers, and artists including Matisse and Picasso, since the nineteenth century. Upon my arrival, the bellboys welcome me as they unhook my Louis Vuitton luggage from the back of the vintage Rolls. Feeling ever the Bond girl, I am escorted into the hotel and immediately given a line of credit at the Casino de Monte-Carlo , where fortunes have been made—and more have been lost—for well over a century. The Casino is the height of chic, designed by Charles Garnier in 1878, and bedecked with magnificent crystal chandeliers, walls lined with gold and painted with frescoes of nude women ... smoking cigars! Juxtaposing mind-boggling luxury with a sense of tradition and fun, Monaco has been ruled by the Grimaldi family for centuries and was, until her untimely death in 1982, the home of the iconic Grace Kelly, who married Prince Rainier in a ceremony that was witnessed the world over, and which gave young girls everywhere the promise that glamorous fairy tales often really do come true. (I know that mine did.)

The most exclusive party in the world begins and ends every year in Monaco during the third or fourth week in May, where, from the deck of a yacht or the balcony of your suite at the Hôtel de Paris, you can witness the heart-stopping Monaco Grand Prix, where on a Saturday afternoon, Formula One cars race through the narrow, winding streets around the world-famous Casino de Monte-Carlo. The city's streets are transformed into the most scenic racetrack in the world, and the cars whirl seventy-eight times around these tight curves at speeds of up to 200 miles per hour. One lap around the entire city takes no more than one minute and twenty-six seconds, and the race itself lasts for about two hours.

People from around the world begin to arrive about a week before the race begins, arriving in gleaming white mega-yachts, bringing their svelte, suntanned bodies to this small Mediterranean Principality to enjoy the pre– and post–Grand Prix festivities that seem to take over everyday life here. The pervasive Mediterranean fragrance of lavender is obscured by the smell of gas and the constant thrum of humming engines, and you feel vibrations through your body as you sip ice-cold champagne. I watch the excitement build, from the balcony of the Hôtel de Paris's Winston Churchill Suite, as handsome H.S.H. Prince Albert II circles overhead in a helicopter, to begin the race.

Traditionally, a special lunch at the hotel's Le Grill or Salle Empire is prepared based on which team you support. In the evening, being admitted to these ultra-exclusive parties sponsored by such racing teams as Ferrari or Mercedes is almost impossible to accomplish and is generally limited to royalty, selected top models, and certain famous actors. Luckily, owning the first-issued McLaren Mercedes Formula One car secures my entrance into the most exclusive party in the world. But, when you live the kosher billionaire lifestyle, anything is possible!

When you're traveling, consider going off-season—during the winter holidays,
for example—when there are not a lot of tourists,
and it's easier to get around in some of the quainter locales.

Entering Les Caves de L'Hôtel de Paris

One winter holiday my husband and I were lucky enough to be in Monte Carlo for what was one of the most romantic and remarkably thrilling nights of my life. Deep beneath the surface of the earth, existing quietly under the Hôtel de Paris, lies a secret, locked wine cave with hidden priceless wine treasures. In the cool dry air of the ancient cave, led along by the hotel's sommelier, we followed a winding path until we came to a locked gate, behind which were dozens of precious, dust-covered vintages that had been hidden by the Monégasques from the pillaging hands of the Nazis during World War II. Here, we were told, Churchill enjoyed his favorite vintages, giving him a brief respite from the war that threatened the world. Some of his cognacs still remain there today behind a locked steel gate. Our visit to the breathtaking space culminated in the greatest surprise of all: a table was set for an opulent dinner, which my husband and I enjoyed in the sanctum of where Prince Rainier and Princes Grace celebrated a special anniversary dinner.

Wherever your travels and your dreams take you, be it Paris or Tuscany, Australia or Brazil, always remember that no matter the menu or the delicious tradition or temptation, you can always maintain your Kosher Billionaire's Secret Recipe! If you're traveling abroad, remember to:

- Enjoy fish (which have scales and fins), but not shellfish
- Delight in the colors and textures of fresh vegetables and fruit
- Relish the wonderful healthy soy-based foods so widely available
- Drink kosher wines and champagnes in moderation
- Drink plenty of bottled water
- And keep moving: walk down the Champs-Élysées, stroll through the museums of Rome and Florence, hike the hills of Provence—just keep moving!

When you return home, you will have enough memories to healthfully feed your heart—and your soul—for a lifetime.

A Tuscan Temptation

From the ancient magnificence that is Florence to the gentle hills of Chianti, Tuscany is an art- and flavor-infused destination for millions of travelers who endeavor to bring back the distinctive tastes for which the area is so well known. Lending themselves easily to adaptation, these wondrous healthy kosher dishes allow me to replicate the dream of being there ... in the luxury of my own home. You will feel as if you're in the misty hills of Tuscany with every delectable morsel.

Menu

Aperitif
Bellinis made with Bartenura Prosecco Extra Dry, Italy

Appetizer
Pizza Vegano
Bartenura Valpolicella 2003, Veneto, Italy

Entrée
Fresh Ricotta and Spinach Ravioli with Parmesan Crème Brûlée
Rashi Select Barolo 2000, Piedmont, Italy

Dessert
Soy Chocolate Mousse with Strawberry Tartar
Bartenura Malvasia 2005, Salento IGT, Italy

Vive la France!

Cuisine is king—and queen—in this magnificent nation of food lovers! Wherever you go in France, be it Paris or Provence, food and wine are central to the day-to-day delicious experiences of its residents and visitors. Enjoy this sumptuous menu as part of the Kosher Billionaire Secret Recipe, close your eyes, and imagine you're at the Ritz!

Menu

Aperitif
Champagne
Laurent-Perrier Brut L-P nv Champagne, France

Appetizer
Vegetable Soup (Potage aux Quatre Saisons)
François Labet Puligny-Montrachet 1er Cru 2004, Burgundy, France

Entrée
Baked Turbot Fillet with Fava Beans and Artichoke Puree
or
Potatoes Maxim with Broccoli Puree
Domaine Pierre Labet Beaune-Coucherias 1er Cru 2004, Burgundy, France

Dessert
Caramelized Apple Cream Puffs
Château Piada Sauternes 2001, Bordeaux, France
or
Louis Royer V.S. Cognac, France

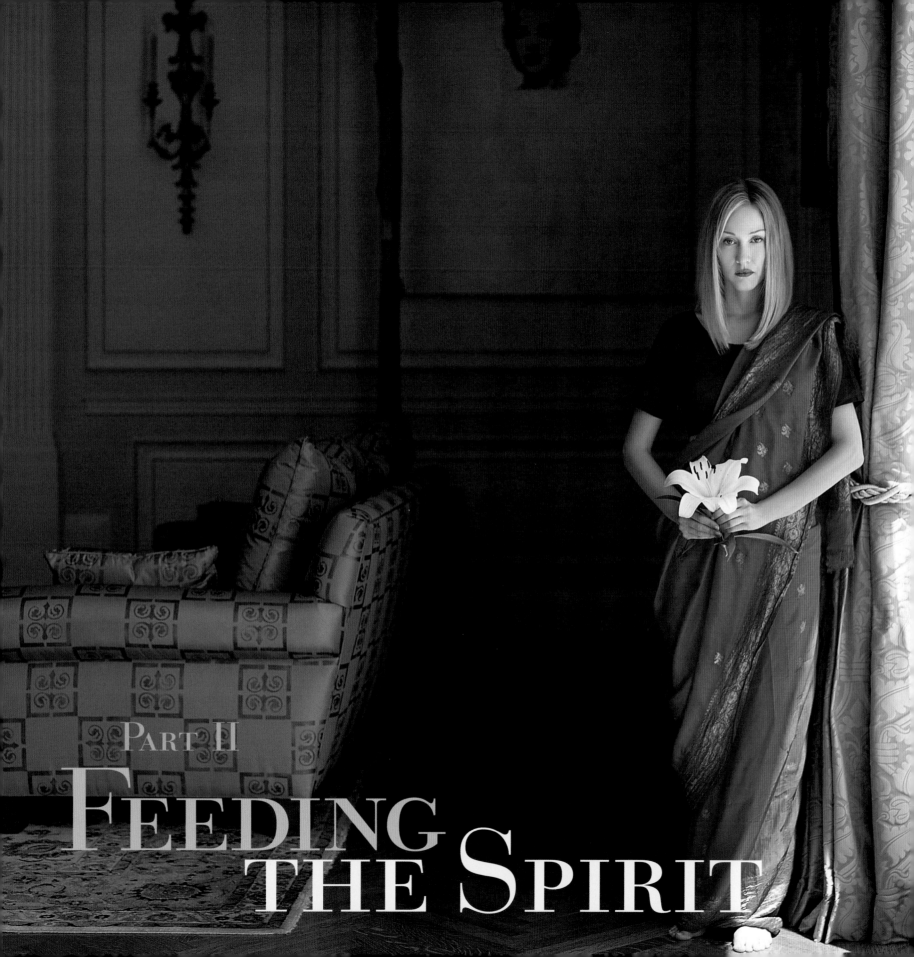

PART II

FEEDING
THE SPIRIT

"Inner peace comes to those who remove judgment from their lives"

CHAPTER IV

THE SECRET RECIPE FOR FINDING YOUR INNER HEALTHY KOSHER BILLIONAIRE

Is it possible to live a spiritually healthy, deeply enlightened life that is connected directly to one's day-to-day existence as a kosher billionaire-in-the-making? To find pleasure in five-thousand-year-old tradition and ritual, to adapt those customs and practices to the kosher billionaire lifestyle, and make life richer, more fulfilling, more prosperous ... and even healthier? Yes, it is! I know this for a fact, because I've done it, and it has affected virtually every portion of my life. The spiritual component is a vibrant, vital part of the Kosher Billionaire's Secret Recipe that just might change the way you, too, view the world, your inner being, and your outer beauty, forever.

"Delicious healthy food is the bond that holds society together."

—STACY COHEN

SLOWING DOWN:
SPIRITUALITY AND THE KOSHER BILLIONAIRE

Come dream with me: sit beside me as we whoosh through the atmosphere, on a journey to far-off cultures and countries. Or join me for a luxurious meal at my dining room table, surrounded by the people I love and care about. Wherever I am, the act of "breaking bread" is, for me, a deeply spiritual experience. The term itself derives directly from a Sabbath ritual, but whether one practices Judaism, Christianity, or any other religion, honoring the Sabbath -taking time to slow down and look within, to honor those who have come before you and will come after, and to give thanks—is all about the mystical act of "taking of bread" in one form or another; this can easily translate to the way we feed ourselves, entertain our loved ones and our guests with heartfelt spirituality, and feed and nurture our souls.

When I began my healthy kosher lifestyle, I did so because I wanted to follow more than 5,700 years of tradition that has its roots in the sacred texts and laws of Judaism; no matter where I am or what I am doing—from my beloved Monaco to Sydney, from India to St. Moritz—my spiritual side is deeply nurtured by the knowledge that my practice not only forces me to slow down and to step, just for a moment, off the fabulous and exciting whirlwind that is my life, but it also directly impacts my health, and well-being, and ultimately creates a far more pleasurable existence for me. So how do I maintain my spiritual nature? Simple: by following the Kosher Billionaire's Secret Recipe!

Learning from the Mystics: Understanding the Kabbalah

In a world that is filled with spiritual natures of different kinds, the centuries-old mysticism of the Kabbalah
is an endless source of fascination and learning for me.
Traditionally, kabbalists, who study and read works by the great kabbalist rabbis and teachers through the centuries
as presented in the Zohar, spend much of their time helping others, giving to charity,
and using their teachings to spiritually uplift and aid the downtrodden.
The Zohar teaches that in order to reach personal fulfillment and enlightenment,
we must resolve to do all we can to become the best people we can possibly be.
The Kosher Billionaire's Secret Recipe works hand in hand with the teachings
of the kabbalist mystics and the Zohar to help you attain spiritual and physical fulfillment,
to look and feel your best, to care for others with profound respect and understanding,
and to treat your body like a temple.

The Kosher Billionaire's Spiritual Journeys, and the Sacredness of Eating Well

Wherever my travels have taken me, I have never had any problem maintaining my healthy kosher lifestyle, and wherever your travels take you, you'll make the same discovery! There is really no better way than through travel to learn how wonderful people all over the world are, how willing they are to understand and learn more about the Kosher Billionaire's Secret Recipe, and it's always a kick to see how surprised they are when they taste the delicious healthy kosher meals that I prepare for them back home.

Maintaining Your Healthy Kosher Lifestyle ...
In Someone Else's Home (or Country!)

Imagine yourself traveling the world in your own private aircraft,
flying from destination to magnificent destination, and making friends and connections wherever you go.
Surely you will be invited to their home to break bread, and enjoy a meal with them!
But how do you maintain your healthy kosher lifestyle when you don't know whether the meal you're about to eat
is either kosher ... or healthy?! First, don't panic!
The trick is to gently find out beforehand what the meal is going to entail and,
if they're not serving kosher beef or chicken, to politely request a vegetarian meal or fish.
If you know in advance how many courses the host is having,
you can balance what you eat accordingly, and enjoy everything.

Some destinations, by their very nature, and because their connection to spirituality is a part of their daily existence, inspire me enormously, and encourage and nurture me to be the best that I can be, to help others, and to live life to its fullest. And the very best part of my travels to these destinations is the memories I bring back home; they are the most sacred souvenirs, along with recipes I adapted so that I can enjoy those foods and memories again in my own home.

Stacy's Sexiest Destinations

Whether you're there for a day, a week, or a month, these destinations are well worth the price of admission in sheer steaminess alone. Take your honey and run—don't walk—on the trip of a lifetime, to Anguilla, Bangkok, Portofino, Monte Carlo, Paris, Rome, Sydney, Jerusalem, St. Moritz, and Santorini.

How can you bring a bit of Japan into your home? Do what I do:
when serving a Japanese meal, I enjoy wearing my silk, Asian-inspired Roberto Cavalli dress
and Japanese hair barrette. It's just a little bit of Kyoto in the privacy of my home.

Japan is an interesting amalgam of quiet countryside, exciting cities, ancient colorful tradition, Zen mysticism, and the most modern technology. With a cuisine renowned for its esthetics (perfect for a kosher billionaire!) and interesting, colorful plate designs, it is also an extremely healthy one: the large majority of Japanese eat fish daily—sometimes several times a day—in the form of sushi (raw fish with vinegar-seasoned rice) or sashimi (raw fish, au naturel).

Just as the sumo wrestlers throw salt into the ring to ward away evil spirits,
I have eliminated salt from our diets to ward away high blood pressure!

If you want to seduce the samurai (Japanese warrior) at your table,
I recommend you try the gold standard for sake, Ken, by the Suehiro Sake Brewery.
Ken is Japanese for sword.

Because it is commonly known that some Westerns fear eating raw fish, the Japanese will usually show a lot of interest in whether or not their American guests choose to eat sashimi, sushi, or a dish that's been cooked. On a recent trip there, I began my meal with some delicious sake; I enjoyed eating their yellowtail, which I delicately dipped into soy sauce, just as my host did.

For dessert, I was surprised to discover how much I enjoyed traditional egg sushi—a perfect way to have a few calories but virtually no fat.

Colorful, healthy, and ancient, the world of Japanese dining and entertaining is a subtly opulent way to live the Kosher Billionaire's Secret Recipe. A few other ways of bringing home your journey to the Far East, wherever you live, is to:

- Serve sake and other Japanese specialties on Asian-inspired dishware and cups, and with magnificent Japanese enameled chopsticks, widely available.
- Buy edamame (Japanese soy beans, and a favorite of mine), and leave them on the vine; place them upright in a bowl of shaved ice as if they were ancient trees set against the snow-capped Japanese mountains. Edamame is commonly available in Asian or American markets.
- When you enjoy sushi or sashimi, do as the Japanese customarily do, and try not to add wasabi to your soy sauce, or pour large amounts of soy into the small dipping plate, as many Americans do. Instead, pour carefully and in small quantities. Japanese food is all about natural flavor, moderation, and health ... just like the Kosher Billionaire's Secret Recipe!

A BILLION-DOLLAR JAPANESE DINNER

Recently I was asked to join a famous Japanese billionaire as his guest at a special dinner. Little did I know that, at this very special tasting, I would be treated to eighteen courses of the most delicious, unusual Japanese foods plated in the most interesting presentations. The first course began with a spoon filled with a soft, white substance, and a hollowed-out egg beside it. The waiter smiled and watched as I cautiously investigated the spoon. "After you eat it, I will tell you what it is," he said—and I carefully slurped it up (in a manner similar to the way the Japanese slurp noodles ... a noisy affair when the food is top-notch). The waiter then told me that they wanted the meal to start out with a little "trick" for the palate—something totally unexpected: to my delight, what was on the spoon was very similar to my beloved panna cotta. The ice was broken, and the courses just kept coming—from the marvelous skewered smelts to the main course of sea bass, the experience was a stunning journey through the world of new and exciting tastes and textures, all of which fit perfectly into my healthy kosher lifestyle!

Most of the delicious foods native to this region appears in the Bible,
from fish to fruit to olive oil to wine!

"Thy plants are an orchard of pomegranates, with pleasant fruits: camphor, spikenard, and saffron, calamus and cinnamon, with all trees of frankincense, myrrh and aloes, with all the chief spices."

— FROM THE SONG OF SOLOMON

ISRAEL:
THE LAND OF MILK AND HONEY

From the glorious ancient cities of Jerusalem and Tel Aviv to the Golan Heights, and magnificent, sun-dappled Elat, there is nothing—really, nothing—that comes close to the spiritual experience of a journey to the Land of Milk and Honey: Israel. People of many faiths come here, to the most diverse and religious nation in the world, to absorb the pulsating history in the air, to worship however they may and however they like, and to enjoy foods fit for King David.

In all of my world travels, I have found nothing comparable to being in Jerusalem and staying at the magnificent King David Hotel. With the early-morning lights just beginning to flicker in this city older than time, I stepped out on my balcony overlooking the Old City and gazed at the city walls, which have protected and encapsulated this birthplace of spirituality for thousands of years. I felt as though I were in King David's presence as I walked the ancient streets; one night, I prayed at the wall of Jerusalem, and asked God for His blessings. Touching or kissing the wall—its limestone always cool on even the hottest summer day—is an incomparably powerful experience. In this ancient country, the people are among the most giving and generous in the world, a sweet spirituality swirls around you, and the foods that are native to the region are among the most naturally healthy available anywhere.

Be sure to add a touch of olive oil and a squeeze of lemon to your hummus, for a bright punch of flavor. Here you can find olive trees that are more than two thousand years old.

Of nearly all the countries I've visited, Israel is perhaps the simplest destination if you are hoping to celebrate your innate spirituality within the Kosher Billionaire's Secret Recipe. Most of the delicious foods native to the region have appeared in one form or another in the Bible, from fish to fruit to olive oil to wine! Combine this with the fact that you'll doubtless be touring thousands of historical sites, and you have an exciting country to visit, packed with wonderful people and delicious, healthy kosher food. It's an easy way to keep your waistline trim and your palate excited!

THE SACRED MARRIAGE OF FOOD AND SPIRIT

Dieting is often boring, which is why so many people fail at it. But I've found that one of the secrets to success in staying healthy is also staying spiritual ... and with the Kosher Billionaire's Secret Recipe, what you'll enjoy eating is directly connected to a tradition more than 5,700 years old, one that began in Israel. From the sprawling breakfast buffet at the King David Hotel, replete with succulent cheeses and even a breakfast salad including fresh vegetables of every kind and color, to ample yet healthy lunches of traditional Israeli salads— small plates no bigger than the palm of your hand, and including vegetables, salads, fruits, honey, yogurt, fish, olives, hummus, and the freshest and most delicious pita available anywhere—it is simple to maintain the healthy kosher lifestyle while taking in the awe-inspiring history that surrounds you everywhere you turn.

Dazzling textures, colors, and flavors fill every market stall and every plate: the result is not only good for your body but great for your spirit. Some of the more spectacularly healthy Israeli dishes include:

- Tabbouleh: cracked bulgur wheat and parsley salad, often served with lemon and chopped fresh tomato and scallion
- Baba ganoush: warm roasted eggplant mashed into a paste and seasoned with lemon, cumin, mint, and parsley, and drizzled with olive oil
- Hummus: a luscious puree of chickpeas and tahini (sesame seed paste), softened with lemon, olive oil, garlic, with cumin or paprika, and sprinkled with a drop of olive oil
- Fish: the freshest fish in Israel comes from the stunning seaside town of Haifa, and includes dorado (known in other parts of the world as mahimahi), bass, and other healthy, white-fleshed fish that are perfect for roasting, sautéing, steaming, or grilling.

Eating in Israel is both a gastronomical and healthy experience all at the same time and enlightens the soul as well as warms the stomach!

"There are no limitations to personal enlightenment."

—STACY COHEN

Personalizing the Kosher Billionaire's Secret Recipe

From Israel to Japan to California, in all the spiritual worlds I visit, it is vitally important to me to feed my spirit via the eons-old culinary traditions of keeping kosher, and you can too! The result will be a healthier, happier, more amazing-looking you! So join me as we continue on our journey together to some of the sexier spiritual spots I've experienced in my secret, healthy kosher billionaire lifestyle. Let your spirit soar with the tingle of these exotic yet satisfying flavors and textures.

A Taste of the Far East

Japanese menus tend to be balanced, packed with natural flavors rather than sauces, and therefore extremely healthy. Here the seitan salad combines delicate and bold flavors of the East and makes a lovely contrast with the elegant main dish.

Menu

Aperitif
Sake
Suehiro Ken "Sword" Daiginjo Sake, Japan

Appetizer
Pan-Seared Seitan Salad
Weinstock Cellar Select Sauvignon Blanc 2005, Central Coast, California

Entrée
Sautéed Lingcod with Vegetable Tartar
François Labet Meursault 1er Cru Clos Richemont 2004, Burgundy, France

Dessert
Tiramisù

THE LAND OF MILK AND HONEY

Israel is the proverbial gastro-ethnic melting pot: at once wholesome, delicious, luxurious, and sensual, its foods sing of ancient ritual, of figs and lemons, milk and honey, of King David and meals that would make royalty (and a kosher billionaire) beg for more! If you want real Isreali style, serve these dishes in small plates and let your guests sample a bit of everything. These tasting-style menus are sure to please and delight new and old friends alike.

Menu

Aperitif
Mishka Vodka Martinis with Kedem Dry Vermouth

Appetizers
Whole Wheat Pita with Hummus*
Fresh Herbed Couscous with Feta and Orange
White and Green Asparagus Salad with Citrus Lavender Vinaigrette
Tempeh Braised in White Wine with Garlic and Fresh Herbs
Eggplant Burgers**
Backsberg Chardonnay 2003, Paarl, South Africa
Verbau Gewürztraminer 2001, Alsace, France
Herzog Special Reserve Merlot 2002, Alexander Valley, California

Dessert
Roasted Figs with Fromage Blanc and Red Wine
Fresh fruit

* Commercially available
**Double or triple this recipe and create smaller,
appetizer-sized burgers.

SEXY
SPIRITUALITY

"Stop to smell the roses:
take walks, read, enjoy the journey of life."

—Stacy Cohen

CHAPTER V

THE KOSHER BILLIONAIRE'S GUIDE
TO SENSUAL JOURNEYS

The setting sun sparkles off the long reflecting pond in front of the buildings, and their white hue is ghostlike in the early-evening light. Before you stands a spiritual gift of love so divine that it has actually earned the name the Shrine of Love; it is the Taj Mahal, built by Shah Jehan over a period of twenty-two years beginning in 1631, in honor of his favorite wife, Mumtaz Mahal, who died giving birth to their fourteenth child, was devoted to her husband, and had accompanied him into battle, as was the Indian custom at the time. The northern part of this brilliantly colorful country is inhabited by an incredible one billion people speaking eighteen different languages, including Hindi, Urdu, Assamese, Bengali, Manipuri, Punjabi, Sanskrit, Sindhi, Tamil, and even English.

Several thousand miles away sits a sparkling, mile-deep caldera, and above it is perched a bleached-white village on a cliff as old as time itself. It is Santorini, where for millennia, the descendants of Greeks who invented math, science, philosophy, drama, and, if one reads the epic poem the Odyssey, love itself, dine on the freshest tomatoes and feta, dolmades (stuffed grape leaves), and mezze to be found anywhere-with a lusty and vigorously healthy spirituality unparalleled anywhere ... except perhaps Spain or Hawaii!

Sensuality and living the best, most amazing life you can; sensuality and the spirit; from the Bible's Song of Solomon to the Kama Sutra, sensuality and spirituality have long been a deeply inseparable, delicious facet of la dolce vita. Ask anyone who glows with sensuality what, exactly, their key is, and they'll likely respond, "It's knowing how to live the good life ... and knowing how to enjoy it." And the good life—no matter how devout or pious you may be—involves the understanding that an amazing life is also an enormously, gratifyingly sensual one, and that living by the healthy secret recipe will leave you feeling awake and alive in a way that perhaps you've never felt before. But how? I'll tell you. Are you ready to continue with me on the exciting journey of a lifetime?

125

Wear gold jewelry: Traditionally, Indian women wear gold jewelry against their skin at all times. From earrings, bracelets, and bangles, to rings for fingers and toes, and even ankle bracelets—gold jewelry is the must-have accessory in the Indian wardrobe. Formerly a symbol of a family's wealth and the dowry it paid at the time of a daughter's wedding, gold jewelry is beloved from north to south. You'll never see an Indian lady without it ... and you shouldn't be seen without it either!

The good life involves the understanding that spirituality can also be enormously, gratifyingly sensual, that living the healthy kosher life will leave you feeling awake and alive in a way that perhaps you've never felt before!

THE SPICY, SENSUAL KOSHER BILLIONAIRE'S SECRET RECIPE

Living a sensual life—with all its delicious tastes, smells, and tactile sensations—is key to the Kosher Billionaire's Secret Recipe. Have you ever bitten into the most delectable, perfectly ripe peach, or nibbled on an indescribably ideal piece of mango? Or touched a magnificent Hermès scarf made of the finest silk available and glowing, intense colors out of a dream? Have you experienced the perfect sunset, run your toes through the warm white sands of Sardinia, or gazed longingly at a superlative painting that you'd only seen in books before? All of those are deeply meaningful, spiritual experiences that may forever change the way you look at the world and add a little bit of spice to your life.

India is one of the most sensual countries in the world; the foods are layered with spices and chilies hot enough to make you cry, and the beautiful, friendly people wear an incredible array of colors in their day-to-day lives. Here, as nowhere else in the world, one can be overwhelmed by sexy, steamy sensory stimulation. The foods of India are as varied as the people, from fiery-hot, curried, coconut-laden vegetarian dishes famous in the southern part of the country, to the delicious chapatis, rotis, and dals of the north. But India is far more than just its luscious, healthy, often vegetarian food; it's all about tradition and a gorgeous array of colors that show up in the most interesting places—in fashion, in one's home, everywhere! And you too can re-create the elegance, glamour, and romance that has swirled around the Taj Mahal for hundreds of years. Here are a few tips for living as if you're entertaining the most prominent raj in town:

Fill your life with color. Don't be afraid to embrace dazzling "jewel" tones like reds, oranges, magentas, and turquoise. Drape beautifully textured fabrics around your favorite pieces of furniture, stock up on pashmina shawls in unexpected hues, lay a brightly colored, lightweight dhurrie on your dining room floor—over your existing rug or carpet—before you have guests over for a lavish dinner. (And simply roll it up and store it for the next Indian-style celebration you have.)

A famous Hollywood power couple, Penélope Cruz, and many other familiar faces ... what a fabulous, exciting combination of celebrity philanthropists dedicated to the art of "giving back." When they decided to put on a benefit to raise money for orphan girls in India, Ricky Martin agreed to sing in order to get this star-power crowd to start bidding on colorful designer gowns modeled by supermodels. Even I couldn't help getting into the spirit by winning a bidding war on a gorgeous black Valentino gown modeled by megamodel Cindy Crawford. The night a success, and everyone looked fabulous in their colorful saris and bold pashminas ... and the Indian food served made us all feel like Hindu royalty.

Billy Crystal's Saturday Night Live *character once said, "Baby, if you look good, you'll feel good!" He was right! Allowing yourself to breathe in and absorb your surroundings—living la dolce vita and all it has to offer—will make you look terrific and feel terrific! So live it up whenever you can. The results will be instantly noticeable!*

"Whatever your imagination can dream, you can become."

—STACY COHEN

THE MODERN ALLURE OF ANCIENT TRADITION

Would you like to live among the likes of Aristotle Onassis and Jackie O., Marilyn Monroe, Maria Callas, and Frank Sinatra, as they sailed through the azure-blue Aegean Sea aboard the famous yacht *The Christina O*? Would you like to bask in the warm, gentle glow of the Mediterranean sun, or stroll on the same sand that was the playground of the first Olympic athletes, before feasting on mouthwatering healthy kosher mezze and dancing the night away with your handsome hunky kosher billionaire beside you? You can!

From the sun-bleached island of Santorini to the bustling boutiques of Athens's Kolonaki Square, Greece lays claim to more ancient sensuality, spirituality, glitz, glamour, sexy mythology, and delectable food than nearly any other place on earth. For thousands of years, it was the cradle of civilization and today, sprawling with history, fun, fabulously healthy food, and more than a small dose of great attitude that comes from knowing that Greek civilization is one of the oldest in recorded history, Greece is a fabulous, sexy destination. These perpetually happy people will teach you that no matter where you are—on the magnificent *Christina O*, or in the privacy of your own home—you can have a happy, beautiful life. It all starts with a great outlook!

When the boisterous, exciting music begins to play at a Greek-themed dinner party, anything can happen ... and it usually does! So if a plate is accidentally broken (or thrown into the fireplace, as is tradition), rather than becoming irate, do as the Greeks do: applaud and exclaim, "'Opa!" Having a great attitude is half the battle of having a happy life!

Right alongside the innately great attitude in Greece is the fact that the country is also the birthplace of healthy Mediterranean cuisine, which can be the focal point of the healthy kosher lifestyle. Nibble on some delectable spanakopita (spinach and cheese baked under a blanket of flaky phyllo dough) or finish dinner with a small piece of honey-drenched baklava; but what better way to start a Greek meal than to do as the gods and goddesses did, and have your love peel you a grape and feed it to you while you lounge on a chaise in a Greek vineyard, or on the beach, with the bright blue water sprawled like a blanket before you? Greek food is fit for the deities who ruled from Olympus ... and for a kosher billionaire!

FOOD FIT FOR THE GODS, GODDESSES ... AND YOU!

Studies have proven time and again that a Mediterranean-style diet is possibly the healthiest and most delicious you can eat; rich in local, seasonal vegetables, brightly colored fruits, grains, and fish, it is virtually synonymous with the Kosher Billionaire's Secret Recipe! Nowhere is the fish fresher, the vegetables in more ample supply, and the wines so delicious—be it Provence, Italy, or Greece. On a typical Greek menu, you'll find small, shareable dishes, called mezze, which might include roasted eggplant and red pepper, warm flatbread drizzled with olive oil (made from thousand-year-old olive trees!), tzatziki (a velvety delicious yogurt dip blended with mint, cucumber, garlic, and olive oil), cheeses that can be grilled in chunks, and larger main course dishes that can include charcoal-grilled souvlaki on a skewer and then served in a warm whole wheat pita, or whole local fish that's been rubbed with garlic and olive oil and grilled (and then filleted for you at your table). Dessert is often the richest part of the meal, with mouthwatering baklava—layered phyllo with nuts and honey—appearing everywhere in smaller, manageable portions! So go ahead ... eat like the gods!

Learning traditional Greek or any local dancing is a fantastic way to exercise! Your arms will receive a workout if you can throw a disk like the Olympic athletes, or even just a plate into a blazing fire at a local restaurant. (But be prepared for the broken plates to be added to your bill!)

131

It's a snap to stay healthy and happy and tan and sexy here,
all while dreaming of that slow and gentle cruise on a private yacht once owned by Ari Onassis.

OUR BIG FAT HONEYMOON ...
ON THE *Christina O*!

If you want to live a full, robust life and make your wildest dreams come true, the best way to be inspired is by exploring the lush and ancient Mediterranean by sea, preferably aboard a private yacht. But not just any private yacht: the lavishly appointed *Christina O*, purchased by shipping magnate Aristotle Onassis, christened for his daughter Christina in 1954, and completely refurbished to be the most elegant private yacht in the world. Considered Onassis's private "floating home" from 1954 to 1975, the yacht played host to more than a few celebrities, including Marilyn Monroe, Elizabeth Taylor, Frank Sinatra, Eva Perón, Winston Churchill, and Maria Callas; and if Greece doesn't inspire enough romance on its own, the yacht was also the site of the wedding celebration of Prince Rainier and Princess Grace of Monaco, as well as Jackie Kennedy and Aristotle Onassis himself! Since this romantic legacy leaves such a remarkably mythical and passionate feeling, I felt that the legendary vessel would be a perfect place on which to celebrate my honeymoon. We boarded to sail the Greek isles right after the 2004 Olympics. What could be more inspiring?

What better way to start a Greek meal than to do as the gods and goddesses did,
and have your beloved half peel you a grape and feed it to you while you lounge on a chaise in a Greek vineyard,
or on the beach, with the bright blue water sprawled like a blanket before you?

A Delicious Olympic Competition

The first Olympic Games were held in Olympia in 776 B.C., and the first modern Olympics were held in Athens in 1896, in a stadium that stands to this day on a broad, palm tree–lined boulevard. In ancient Greece, athletic events were viewed as a sort of religion based on human strength, vigor, and the beauty of the human form. I was inspired to want to be in the best shape of my life after watching the athletes perform. It was deeply inspiring to watch Michael Phelps as he swam for a record-breaking eight medals—six of them gold—and received them on the podium under the American flag. Taking a tour of the Panathenaic Stadium gave me the feeling that the Olympiads of the past were still very much alive. (Of course, the Olympic runners no longer streak around the track as the Greeks did, in the nude -although it certainly would be an incentive to tone quickly!)

One way to maintain that healthy competitive edge is to take it out to dinner! The next time you're in a restaurant with a group of friends, make it a point to compete to see who orders the best dish!

As we steamed along the Mediterranean with the benevolent ghosts of Ari and Jackie as our guides, onward in the magnificent vessel, toward the breathtaking white cliffs and whitewashed chapels of Santorini, we were accompanied by a pod of dolphins—some of the most spiritually attuned creatures on earth—who seemed to recognize that their onlookers were celebrating the most important time of their lives as newlyweds! As if to exclaim "congratulations," the leader of the pod raced the bow of the boat before doing a flip and swimming away.

From historically captivating Crete and the legendary Palace of Knossos to the low-key, undeveloped island of Symi, which was the perfect place for a loving couple to dream of their future together, Greece was one of the most stunning destinations I have had the privilege of visiting. We concluded our journey on the island of Patmos, where we enjoyed one of my favorite comfort foods, avgolemeno, the warm and soothing Greek rice soup made with egg and lemon. Even the charming Greek grandmothers who told our fortunes from the coffee grounds in the bottom of our cups could see what lay before us: happiness, health, peace, and love.

How can you bring the spirit of the Olympics to your home? By bringing competition into your kitchen, striving to do your best, and making the most healthy kosher recipes you can!

"From early morning
until the darkest hour, it often seems that Spain never sleeps!"

—STACY COHEN

THE HEALTHY KOSHER BILLIONAIRE'S CHALLENGE:
LIVING AND EATING IN SENSUAL SPAIN

Thrilling, romantic, pulsating, and filled to the brim with stunning people who are deeply passionate about everything from food to politics to fashion, Spain is one of the greatest sensory experiences on earth, just ripe for a visit from a healthy kosher billionaire engaged in all of the opulent things that life has to offer: they can all be found here, in Spain.

Imagine that you have awakened in the seaside metropolis of Barcelona, where the sweet but heavy Mediterranean air lies like a blanket on the city, already alive with the vibrant early-morning traditions of *churros*, sweet batter-based pastry sticks that are often dipped into chocolate, and café con leche (black coffee poured over sugar and heated milk), taken not only as a form of nourishment but also as a way to wake up from the previous night's dancing and socializing with these remarkably friendly, accommodating people (thankfully, the Spaniards love their coffee almost as much as their delicious wines). At about eleven, another mid-morning breakfast is enjoyed by everyone: *bocadillos*, or small sandwiches, stem hunger pangs that come from walking everywhere, taking in the magnificent ancient sites, and the sheer energy of the place.

When in Spain, work off extra calories by doing what I did: see Picasso's work at the museums in Barcelona; visit Madrid and stroll through the Prado, whose heavy walls hold treasures for all to see, from Velázquez to Goya, and beyond. And be sure not to miss Joan Miró's magnificent work.

The people of Spain are incredibly friendly, giving people, and so when I asked some locals at a *chiringuito*—or beach bar—where the best places to eat dinner were located, they not only told me: they invited me to join them! That evening, I donned my red Valentino dress that was perfect for a sultry night out in this sensual country. Arriving at the local tavern at around 11:30 p.m., my night was just beginning: through the reddish glow, I was greeted by the *castanettas*, sexy cabaret dancers who seem to be eternally in motion; they escorted me to a large, round table of twelve, beautiful sophisticated Spaniards—my new friends whom I'd met earlier in the day! The night began with great conversation, and we dined on traditional tapas—small plates of a wide variety of delicious, local foods—and Spanish almond-flavored sherry.

The custom of eating tapas originated in Andalusia in the nineteenth century, when the bartenders would put out small plates of local cheeses, olives, and often marinated vegetables for their patrons. Over the years, the tradition became more lavish, and now includes dishes of *piperade*, an open-faced, colorful Basque-style omelet laden with red, green, and yellow peppers; marinated tuna; the original Spanish omelet—*tortilla espãnola*—stuffed with potatoes; and much, much more. Whatever is served, it is always based on what is fresh, local, and indigenous to the region. The evening I had with the people of Spain will make me smile forever.

The Joy of Coming Home

You've just experienced a whirlwind journey that married colors and textures to a kaleidoscope of flavors and thriving spirituality, and now you're coming home. Your mind lingers over the glorious destinations to which you'll return over and over again, to enjoy the voluptuous tastes, exciting people, and fabulous sites you've experienced from one side of the globe to the other.

Coming home—wherever it may be and however you may get there—conjures up images of comfort, indulgence, and the delicious tastes of the secret recipe lifestyle your way. Who says that returning to your home, wherever you're from, can't also be luxuriously seductive and wildly exotic? It is! And this is a part of what rounds out the spiritually sensual experience of travel abroad: coming home can be just as spectacular a sensory experience as a four-Michelin-star dinner overlooking Paris!

WHAT IS THE SPANISH CHALLENGE?

I always recommend that wherever you go, you follow the customs of each country you visit.
But what happens when you are a guest in a country like Spain, which is so in love with its food that the average
Spaniard eats four to five times a day, culminating with a late-night meal after a few hours of dancing and socializing?
Will it wreak havoc on the Kosher Billionaire's Secret Recipe? Absolutely not! The Spanish solve this challenge
by eating their main meal during the day, walking nearly everywhere, and dancing as much as they can!
A few tips for maintaining the healthy lifestyle while you're in the land of Picasso and Balenciaga include:
Begin your day, as the Spaniards do, with a sweet churro and a cup of café con leche.
Walk everywhere: stroll through the museums, meander the streets, window-shop to your heart's content.
Enjoy a healthy lunch and an afternoon snack.
Try to have smaller, lighter dinners, and if you can't help but indulge in a typically Spanish late-evening meal,
burn some calories enjoyably: Make love to your spouse!
Not only do these tips solve the Spanish challenge, they will bring a long-lasting smile to your face.
They certainly work for the Spanish!

A Warm Kosher Billionaire Aloha

One of the most strikingly sensual American destinations is one that is also healthy, fresh, colorful, and steeped in the mélange of traditions that make the Kosher Billionaire's Secret Recipe such a rich tapestry of experiences. As you soar above the bright blue Pacific, you see her: the American island chain that we call Hawaii, where life itself seems to stand still, the pace slows to a near halt, and everything around you—from the sand to the surf to the people—seems to have stepped out of the movie South Pacific.

Here, in Hawaii, more than fourteen delicious cultures are woven together in peace, resulting in a magnificent fabric composed of native Hawaiians, Chinese, Japanese, Samoans, Filipinos, African-Americans, Eskimos, Tahitians, Tongans, Portuguese, Spanish, Puerto Rican, Korean, and "Haole" (white people), all of whom not only live side by side with each other: they welcome guests with open arms. The traditional flower lei greeting is only the start of a mystical, magical stay that will have you wanting to return again and again to a place where it's easy to eat delectable kosher foods that are the freshest and possibly the most flavorful on earth. From fish that has been plucked from the bright blue waters moments before being served, to nectar-packed tropical fruits and succulent vegetables, it is downright easy to maintain the kosher billionaire lifestyle in this stunning American wonderland.

A Bit of Hawaii at Home, Kosher Billionaire Style

It's simple and delightful to re-create the Hawaiian lifestyle, wherever you are. Your *akami* (clever) *malahinis* (newcomers and guests) will love it!
- Bring fresh, exotic flowers—birds of paradise, orchids, hibiscus—into your home; place them in vases, put them out on the deck, float the blossoms in glass bowls, and watch *South Pacific* come alive!
- Put on some Hawaiian-style slack-key guitar CDs, to help you get in the mood.
- Treat yourself to a tight-fitting, stunning Hawaiian floral muumuu, and welcome your partner home with a glass of champagne, take his shoes and socks off at the door, and let his kosher billionaire Hawaiian fantasy begin!
- Set up candles wherever you can that's safe, lower the lights, and imagine the sound of the surf and the tastes and textures of a healthy kosher pu pu (appetizer) platter!

A Fragrant Welcome

A deeply welcoming and spiritual people, the ancient Hawaiians began stringing leis to present to each other as "gifts of adornment"—wearing one (or several) was thought to greatly enhance one's natural beauty, vigor, and even sexual prowess. Today they are placed around the necks of all arriving visitors as a symbol of love and welcoming friendship.

The soft fragrance of tuberoses filled the air as my husband and I sat down for a luscious Hawaiian sunset dinner near the clear, turquoise Pacific. We nibbled our last bite of delicate and buttery mahimahi and took a moment to hold hands and gaze at the magnificent infinity of the ocean. Suddenly, as if in response to the deeply spiritual and romantic moment that we were experiencing, a great plume of water arose in the air, and we watched in amazement as a mammoth humpback whale breached. Before our eyes, she burst through the water, made a joyful midair twist, and fell onto her belly, making an enormous splash. We quickly removed our shoes and ran to the water's edge to get a closer look, and were treated to one of nature's greatest miracles: a whale calf following its mother's breach. My husband put his arms around me, and the moments passed in silence as we watched this priceless display of power, exuberance, and love, over and over again.

By lighting a few tiki torches, laying down a track or two of slack-key guitar music, and wearing an aloha shirt or a lei, you'll get into that wonderfully relaxed Hawaiian frame of mind in a heartbeat! With a Mai Tai, you'll get there in the fast lane!

Ask anyone who glows with sensuality what exactly their key is,
and they'll likely respond, "It's knowing how to live the good life ... and knowing how to enjoy it."

California Dreamin', The Kosher Billionaire Way

Sometimes the most sumptuous escapes are right around the corner, and if you're lucky enough to live in the great state of California, you know exactly what I mean! Closest in lifestyle, food, and wine to the glitzy and glamorous Mediterranean, California has taught the rest of America how to live la dolce vita for nearly two centuries by now. From the northern part of the state, where wineries and vineyards dot the fertile countryside and there are as many magnificent vintages and groundbreaking restaurateurs as there are in Burgundy or Tuscany, to the southern part, where, on beaches that rival those of the Côte d'Azur, gorgeous, bikini-clad *Baywatch* babes lounge alongside movie starlets, where the Beach Boys' "California Girls" might as well be the state's anthem, and where trendily spectacular fashion, style, food, and entertaining have been elevated to an art form ... there is no place in the world quite like California.

California is the land of the Gold Rush, a place where dreamers go to make it big, and only those who really believe in the power of success have the fortitude to make it real. If you dream big, like a kosher billionaire, you'll live as a kosher billionaire! In California—and really, no matter where you live—anything is possible!

Of course, one of the greatest gifts that California has given to us (aside from the movie industry, the wine industry, stunning architecture, brilliant musicians, spectacular writers, top-flight universities ... all wrapped in a gorgeous, sun-drenched package), is the American culinary renaissance. Largely thanks to an immensely diverse population, which includes one of the largest Hispanic and Asian populations in the country, California Cuisine is best described as a fusion of styles, textures, flavors, and delicious health. Today, artisanal and organic farms dot the state from north to south, providing top-flight restaurants like Wolfgang Puck's Spago, Thomas Keller's The French Laundry, and Alice Waters's Chez Panisse, with the finest foods available anywhere on the planet. In California, food is treated with reverence, as a great sensual pleasure, and one that is packed with great health benefits.

So join me and live as a kosher billionaire should ... with good health, warm sensuality, striving always to be the best, and with the vibrancy of spirit that all adds up to the Kosher Billionaire's Secret Recipe!

THE STEPS OF POSITANO

On our first Valentine's Day together, my husband invited me to attend a semiprivate Chris Botti concert; he had entered a lottery to win the tickets—and he actually did! Talk about the power of positive thinking! There were only forty people in the audience, so we all had the opportunity to meet this musical master after the performance. And knowing that we fell in love to his music, Chris has entertained us and our celebrity friends on numerous occasions in our home with his seductive smooth jazz. But you don't need to win the lottery to enjoy good luck, just friends and music, and the warmth of sharing.

DINNER WITH MIGHTY APHRODITE

Greek food is some of the lustiest and freshest around, ripe with herbaceous Mediterranean flavors and textures that date back thousands of years to the time of the Greek goddess of love and beauty, Aphrodite. Put on some Greek music, don your finest white handkerchief-linen dress, light the candles, and serve this meal that is sure to intoxicate even the most reserved dinner partner. After dinner, do as the Greeks do, and dance the night and the calories away in a swirl of exuberant high spirits that are sure to follow this zesty menu. *'Opa!*

MENU

Appetizer
Crispy Tofu-Mushroom Phyllo Turnovers
François Labet Corton-Charlemagne Grand Cru 2003, Burgundy, France

Entrée
Roast Stuffed Shoulder of Lamb with Grilled Zucchini and Celery Root Puree
Bodegas Ramón Bilbao Reserva 2001, Rioja, Spain

or

Sautéed Black Sea Bass with White Wine Sauce and
Black Olive and Eggplant Puree
Herzog Special Reserve Chardonnay 2002, Alexander Valley, California

Dessert
Apricot Agrodolce and Vanilla Soy Ice Cream
Sabra Chocolate Orange Liqueur, Israel

The Kosher Billionaire's California Dream

Freshness, color, health, diversity, and intensely delicious flavors are all hallmarks of a gastronomical lifestyle that put California on the culinary roadmap, alongside—and often above and beyond—the finest traditional cuisines in the world. Often copied by other countries, but rarely duplicated, California Cuisine is the way to the kosher billionaire's healthy heart! If you want to really do it California style, make the plate your canvas and arrange the colors and shapes as if you were creating a masterpiece.

Menu

Aperitif
Champagne
or
Los Arango Añejo Tequila Margaritas

Appetizer
Polenta Crostini with Zucchini and Brie
in a Tomato Olive Vinaigrette
Weinstock Cellar Select Sauvignon Blanc 2005, Central Coast, California

Entrée
Fish and Chips
Baron Herzog Rosé of Cabernet 2004, California

Dessert
A Billionaire's Sin
Herzog Late Harvest Riesling 2004, California

PART III

FEEDING
THE HEART

"Helping others is the highest calling, a truly life-affirming experience."

—STACY COHEN

CHAPTER VI

THE KOSHER BILLIONAIRE'S SECRET RECIPE
AND THE ART OF GIVING BACK

Imagine the innocent faces of twenty or thirty children as they listen with rapt attention to the glory of mellifluous symphonic music written in 1936, long before their young, innocent worlds were turned upside-down. You watch them live the music, feel it, embrace it, as the story of *Peter and the Wolf* is recounted to them by a syrup-voiced actor who holds them in the palm of his hand. For a short moment, their troubles are set aside, and they feel nothing but joy, pleasure, happiness, and safety—and you, in loving kindness and compassion, feel a sudden warm glowing sensation in your heart. On a star-studded afternoon filled with interesting wines and delicious foods, you and your party celebrate with abandon, as you have just underwritten a concert and raised funds to help orphans and underprivileged children. At the end of the afternoon, realizing what a success it has been, that same familiar glowing sensation in your heart emerges.

You have just experienced the ageless, timeless endorphin rush that results from philanthropy—giving back to those who have perhaps a bit less than you do, or who might be facing difficult circumstances. Call it what you will: call it a miracle, a gift, or a mitzvah. But whatever you call it or however it manifests itself in your life, it is one of the most important, joyful, life-sustaining, and life-altering components of the Kosher Billionaire's Secret Recipe. Just remember, you don't have to be a billionaire to live like one: the smallest act of giving back can be worth its weight in gold!

Giving back—philanthropy—means many things. It can mean something as small as the touch of a hand, or the grace of entertaining someone in your home and making them feel, if only for one evening, that they are being treated like royalty, fed magnificent foods and wine, being cared for and nurtured.

What's Good for the Giver:
The Surprising Benefit of Giving Back

Whether it's buying Girl Scout cookies from your neighbor's little girl, or volunteering your time once or twice a week to help out a worthy cause, or donning your most stunning Yves Saint Laurent gown and having an all-out charity bash for a cause that's near and dear to your heart, there are some very surprising physical benefits to giving back, and they will not only have an impact on the way you think about philanthropy but will change the way you feel, look, and think about yourself!

Altruism—giving of yourself either materially or emotionally—can have a profound effect on the heart, both literally and figuratively. Studies have repeatedly shown that people who volunteer their time or are actively involved in giving may have reduced blood pressure and cholesterol levels, may experience a greater sense of personal calm and peace, and may have better interpersonal relationships with those they love.

Experiencing
The "Helper's Euphoria"

So, if you get out there and volunteer your time, not only will you be doing a good deed, but you will also enhance your immune system, improve your heart rate, and get a better night's sleep! In a recent study conducted by the University of Michigan, it was actually proven that people live longer when they volunteer. The benefits of giving back are incomparable: altruism actually reduces everyday stress, lessening its impact on your body and mind; you will be able to better cope with change and crisis; and you'll feel more compassion and empathy toward others. There is no diet or exercise regimen that will make you feel quite as good, or give you the same kind of endorphin high. I call this the "Helper's Euphoria." For me, working with philanthropic organizations gives me the same kind of endorphin boost as exercise. I look and feel like a billion bucks after a charity event!

Have you been thinking about doing yoga, or going to a meditation class? You can have the same positive effect on your body by volunteering! According to Harvard cardiologist and expert on relaxation and stress reduction Dr. Herbert Benson, "people have been describing techniques for millennia on how to forget oneself, to experience decreased metabolic rates and blood pressure, heart rate and other health benefits. Altruism works this way, just as do yoga, spirituality and meditation." So instead of going to that yoga class three times a week, cut it down to twice and spend one hour volunteering instead!

"Believe only in action. The smallest act of giving back can often be priceless."

—Stacy Cohen

The Ancient Practice of Tzedakah

Some call it altruism, others call it giving back or philanthropy. This act of giving of yourself either materially or emotionally has roots in a 5,700-year-old Biblical tradition called tzedakah, which is tied directly to living a great and happy kosher billionaire lifestyle! From a very young age, people who practice tzedakah (which translates from the Hebrew as justice or righteousness) instill in their children the same practice; it becomes a daily way of life rather than a special occasion. Very often, children as young as four or five years old keep a little box into which they deposit pennies and nickels, and then send the result to a charity of their choice, or to other children in need. If you've never taken part in tzedakah, it might be fun to try it for a month, and see if your inclination to give back grows with your dollar! The Kosher Billionaire's Secret Recipe expands on tzedakah and includes giving in all ways—whether it be a monetary gift (a gift of money), volunteering of oneself (a gift of time), or an emotional gift (a gift of compassion). All are worthy, and all will result in helping someone in need.

Giving Back ... in Style!

It's always a joy and a thrill to be able to combine two of my favorite things in the world: philanthropy and entertaining. Together, they are an unbeatable combination for getting my "giving endorphins" flowing and my metabolism moving while benefiting some of my favorite causes! No matter what charity you donate your time, compassion, or resources to, or what level of donation you're able to make, you too can give back like a kosher billionaire. It just takes a little planning, a hefty dose of fun, a helping of style, and a big heart!

Among the philanthropic, charity is considered to be a short-term endeavor, and philanthropy a longer-term, generally longer-lasting (and farther-reaching) enterprise. For example, Warren Buffett Jr. gave his fortune to the already established Bill Gates Foundation because he knew that he would be able to leverage his money more quickly, thus achieving his wishes more rapidly.

Any dinner party, luncheon, or tea can be turned into a charity event.
It just takes a little planning, a hefty dose of fun, a helping of style, and a big heart!

Camp Okizu
AND THE GIFT OF GIVING TO CHILDREN

If you're reading this, you may already live the life of a healthy kosher billionaire, or be well on your way! But no matter where you are in the process, you may sometimes feel overwhelmed by life, and wanting to console yourself—as many of us do—with food or shopping or in any of the comforting external trappings that we as humans have come to covet. We all love wonderful clothes, delicious healthy kosher foods that nourish our bodies as well as our souls, and the joys that come with far-off travel to mystical places. But sometimes, external comforts simply aren't enough to quell the doldrums that may hit when we least expect it, and this is totally and completely normal. One of the best ways of dealing with these times is to focus our attention away from ourselves, and onto someone else—and that feeling of emptiness is miraculously replaced with the simple satisfaction of giving. But where to start?

One of the causes I am deeply dedicated to is the research into and treatment of pediatric cancer and blindness. This passion to help children has led to my involvement in Camp Okizu, the largest camp in California designed specifically for kids with cancer and their siblings, with the goal of enhancing their self-esteem, building skills they never thought they'd be able to master ... and just having fun being normal kids! Okizu, which is a Sioux word for "unity," brings kids with cancer together, and shows them that life can be a blast under even the most trying circumstances.

I've always been involved in raising money for charity ever since I was a child, so it was a thrill to be able to experience extreme "Helper's Euphoria" when I bid on an excursion aboard software guru Larry Ellison's yacht. With the proceeds going to help Camp Okizu, I was able to put a smile on the faces of thirty young campers by taking them for a wonderful sail on a cloudless October day. I was surrounded by nothing but beaming young faces when the United States Navy's Blue Angels flew overhead in formation, tipping their wings in a testament to honor the courage and strength of these miraculous children. It was a day that neither they nor I will ever forget!

The limits of philanthropy know no bounds, so if you're planning on either hosting a charity event, partaking in one, or simply volunteering your time, remember that creativity counts! On behalf of Camp Okizu, I've donated the use of my Gulfstream aircraft for philanthropic events, and have had fun bidding on and bringing home items like Sheryl Crow's guitar and a signed Barry Bonds baseball—all for the benefit of children with cancer.

155

How to throw a Fabulous Charity Bash, Big or Small

Think about the possibilities: that dinner engagement you were planning on having can now also result in a nice donation to a fund supporting research for Alzheimer's or AIDS. That funky dinner party it's your turn to host can now also benefit a cancer research fund! Virtually any get-together, with a little bit of planning, can become a charity event. It doesn't have to be fancy ... but it does have to be fun and inspired! If you want to turn your next party into a charity event, call your chosen organization first and ask for some advice on planning; how to collect entry fees; and how to donate them properly to the fund itself. The results will amaze you!

Giving of Your Home:
The Kosher Billionaire's Helping High

The art of giving back is never limited to formal donations, fund-raising parties, writing checks, or even volunteering: by bringing people into your home, entertaining them with style, and offering them a healthy kosher meal, lovely vintage wines, and a wonderful evening—you're still giving of yourself in a manner that will leave them and you glowing, healthier, and happier.

The joy-filled, delicious act of entertaining others, making them feel wonderful, pampered, and nurtured, is a priceless gift, comparable in heartfelt value to the most expensive diamond or the most extravagant gown. Right alongside tzedakah—the ages-old practice of charity—is the importance of bringing guests to your table, to your home, serving them in the most beautiful manner possible, and making sure they have everything they need. There's even a formal statement, spoken during the Passover holiday, that points to feeding "the stranger in your midst." So remember: every opportunity to entertain or to offer a wonderful meal is a joyous gift of love and compassion ... and part of the Kosher Billionaire's Secret Recipe!

A FRENCH AFFAIR

Not that kind of affair, you silly goose! This typically Gallic menu melds together the flavors, aromas, and textures of classic French cuisine, from Normandy in the northern part of the country, to Paris in the central part, to sunny Provence in the south. Serve this delectable kosher treat at a French-themed charity dinner, or anytime!

Menu

Aperitif
Champagne
Laurent-Perrier Brut L-P nv Champagne, France

Appetizer
Hearty Fish Soup Stew with Garlic and Parsley Crostini
Baron Edmond Rothschild Le Rosé de Clarke 2004, Bordeaux, France

Entrée
Assorted cheeses, such as Epoisses, Brillat-Savarin, Morbier*
Château de la Tour Clos de Vougeot 2004, Burgundy, France

Dessert
Caramelized Apple Cream Puffs
Château Piada, Sauternes 2001, Bordeaux, France
or
Louis Royer V.S. Cognac, France

*Commercially available

"Follow your convictions with strength ."

—STACY COHEN

If someone you know is ill, touch their hand, or give them a hug; sometimes this kind of care is worth far more than writing a check to a charity. It can make all the difference for both the receiving party and the caregiver.

CHAPTER VII

FEELING
THE LOVE, LIVING THE LIFE!

The gentle thrum of the aircraft awakens you as you float lightly above the runway, touching down so gently it seems as though you've landed on a cloud. You adjust the powder blue cashmere wrap loosely draped around your shoulders, and remove the black Chanel sunglasses that you bought on that crystal-clear, sun-dappled day in Nice on the Rue de France. The Kosher Billionaire's Secret Recipe is a splendid, never-ending, life-changing journey that's taken you from one end of the globe to the other and back home again, in perfect opulence. It's taken you by the hand and shown you how to rethink the way you live and the way you dine, so that every facet of your life is chock-full of the most amazing experiences of a lifetime, wonderful healthy kosher food that nudges your tastebuds awake out of their culinary doldrums and lavishes upon you not only flavor but delicious health and beauty, no matter where you are! You've swum with presidents and lunched with celebrities, walked in the footprints of gods and goddesses and the samurai, enjoyed marvelous kosher wines and vintage kosher champagne everywhere from Paris to Monaco and Rio to Napa. You've entertained with grace and elegance, welcomed guests into your home with open arms, served succulent meals fit for royalty, and given back to your favorite charities with love and health-giving compassion. In the process, you have become the most mesmerizing person you could possibly be, filled with joy, happiness, light, and good health.

This day, you realize, marks your emergence; it is the beginning of the next phase of your life, where a dream is a goal, just waiting to happen ... only this dream—your dream—has come true.

The secret recipe is no longer really a secret, now that you hold the key to the good life! Instead, it is a way of living, a sensibility that has the capacity to alter who you are at the deepest, cellular level: partaking of the Kosher Billionaire's Secret Recipe, you'll actually now see the world in a different way. It will be brighter, more delicious, more exciting, perhaps filled with more joy and love than you ever thought possible, and dedicated to living la dolce vita! Your journey to the good life has come full circle.

By journeying alongside me, you and I have taken the world by storm! You've slipped on a pair of gorgeous Lacroix pumps and donned that signature red Valentino gown; you've discovered the healthy kosher regimen that allows you to enjoy the finest foods the world has to over, all while maintaining great health and vigorous beauty. My secret recipe is my gift to you, and one that you'll keep near your heart, and use, forever!

Your life will be brighter, more delicious,
more exciting, perhaps filled with more joy and love than you ever thought possible!

Living La Dolce Vita,
The Kosher Billionaire Way!

Thanks to the Kosher Billionaire's Secret Recipe, you've experienced some of the finest foods the world has to offer, but in a manner that leads to great health, and a deep, vibrant glow that comes from within. This groundbreaking regimen, marrying elegant gourmet meals and incredible health to the kosher lifestyle, is the first of its kind anywhere, and will forever change the way you think about dining in, or out; with its help, you too can enjoy dining with pleasure and indulgence ... and without restriction! By following the delectable kosher billionaire lifestyle, you'll also maintain a tradition almost six thousand years old, and do so with an elegance that will wow all of your guests. How many hosts and hostesses can say the same?

My secret recipe for life is so much more than just an exercise in eating well; it's a very personal roadmap to pleasure, peace, joy, and looking and feeling better than you have ever thought possible. It has plaited together the deep, emotional satisfaction that comes with knowing that you've learned how to savor the sweet life, with all its trappings and its goodness ... and that you've also seen that taking care of your spirit, your dreams, and the dreams of others is so vitally important. This is the Kosher Billionaire's Secret Recipe, the recipe for la dolce vita, for the rest of your life!

"Use your gifts and they will increase;
practice what you know, and you will attain higher knowledge."

—STACY COHEN

"Be as you wish to seem."
—Socrates

REACHING YOUR GOALS, CAPTURING THE STARS

Attaining the goals of health, happiness, and loving compassion are never beyond your reach. In fact, nothing is beyond your reach! Remember the kosher billionaire's motto: Reach for the Moon and You'll Capture the Stars!

- *Love the regimen: Enjoy the kosher lifestyle! Eat in moderation but dine well wherever you go, with style, elegance, and class, endeavoring to treat your body like the temple it is.*
- *Live well: Slip on those Manolos and that Cavalli gown, and opt for elegance and luxury whenever and wherever you can. The smallest details and touches can create a big impact, whether you're in the air, flying to some luxurious tropical destination, or in your own home, entertaining your guests with a wonderful feast to celebrate something ... anything!*
- *Celebrate like royalty: There's no reason to have to wait for special occasions to enjoy a magnificent meal with the people you love. That you're together is reason enough, so go ahead: treat them—and yourself—to a meal fit for King David.*
- *Give from the heart: It'll do your own heart a world of good. Compassionate giving works wonders not only for the receiver but for the giver. So whether it's a dollar or a million, hold someone's hand who is in need and watch your inner glow simply beam.*

And always, no matter where you go and what you do ... remember to live la dolce vita!

Mangia e Bevi in Positano, An Italian Seaside Dinner

From Viareggio and south to Positano and Portofino, the Italian Riviera is a quintessentially sun-dappled sandy playground where those who "have it" flaunt it aboard their spectacular yachts. Fresh fish and produce abound here, making a native menu undeniably delicious, healthy, and redolent of the flavors of the sparkling blue sea. If you think of tangy seaside air and gorgeous sunsets unfurling in the clouds, you can bring the Italian seaside right to the table. *Bellissima Italia!*

MENU

Aperitif
Champagne
or
Bellinis made with Bartenura Prosecco Extra Dry, Italy

Appetizer
Vegetable Broth with Artichoke Croutons
Bartenura Pinot Grigio 2005, Provincia di Pavia IGT, Italy

Entrée
Halibut Livornese with Spinach Mashed Potatoes
Toscaleoni Chianti 2003, Tuscany, Italy

Dessert
Chocolate Mousse with Strawberry Tartar
Bartenura Malvasia 2005, Salento IGT, Italy

The Kosher Billionaire's Holiday Dinner

Whatever holidays you celebrate, the key to creating the perfect feast lies in visual and culinary ebullience: always strive to serve celebratory dishes that are rich in flavor and also are truly beautiful. Your guests will love being treated like royalty!

Menu

Aperitif
Champagne
Nicolas Feuillatte Brut nv Champagne, France

Appetizer
Braised Beef Cheeks with Salsa Verde, Horseradish, and Mixed Baby Greens
Lamblin Chablis 1er Cru Vaillon 2002, Burgundy, France

Entrée
Tofu Ragù with Eggplant Timbale with Fresh Pea Puree
Château Yon-Figeac Saint-Émilion 1999, Bordeaux, France

Dessert
Crema Catalana (made with soy)
Château Piada Sauternes 2001, Bordeaux, France

My goal in sharing these delicious recipes with you is twofold: first, quite simply, they are magnificent favorites that are, for the most part, easy to prepare and perfect for every occasion, be it casual or elegant. Second, they are the testament to the fact that it is possible to maintain a healthy kosher lifestyle while eating fabulous dishes worthy of the most gourmet food–loving kosher billionaire (like me!).

It is important to note that absolutely every dairy dish included can be made *pareve* simply by replacing the dairy component with its related, high-quality soy product; in other words, I have used butter substitute or oil exclusively; cheese wherever necessary can be replaced with top-quality soy cheese; and milk—as it appears in dessert recipes and others—should be replaced with full-fat soy milk in order to create *pareve* dishes.

As they say in my beloved Positano, *Mangia bene!*

—Stacy Cohen

Part IV
The Secret Recipes

APPETIZERS
SALADS AND
VEGETABLES

POTATOES MAXIM
WITH BROCCOLI PUREE

Serves 4

This classic culinary combination of potatoes and broccoli is redolent of earthy goodness. Presented as I suggest below, each plate looks like a hibiscus flower. Slice the potatoes on a Japanese-style mandoline to achieve maximum thinness.

For the broccoli puree:
1 teaspoon extra virgin olive oil
1 teaspoon butter substitute
1/4 cup coarsely chopped onion
1 medium potato (about 4 ounces), peeled and coarsely chopped
1/2 garlic clove, chopped
2 cups broccoli florets plus 4 florets for garnish
Kosher salt

1. Heat the oil and butter substitute in a 1- or 2-quart saucepan over medium heat until hot. Add the onion, potato, and garlic and sauté for 2 minutes.
2. Add broccoli, 2 cups water, and 1/8 teaspoon salt. Raise the heat and simmer 5 minutes until the broccoli is tender but not falling apart. Remove 4 florets and set aside. Continue cooking until the broccoli is falling apart and the potato crushes easily against the side of the pan when pressed with the back of a spoon.
3. Transfer the contents of the pan to a blender and puree until smooth. Measure the puree and stir in enough water to equal 1 1/2 cups puree.

For the potatoes:
2 small potatoes, scrubbed and sliced into paper-thin rounds
Extra virgin olive oil
Kosher salt and freshly ground black pepper

1. Preheat the oven to 375 degrees F. Cut four 4-inch squares of parchment paper. Lightly brush with oil. Lay 8 slices of potato in a concentric circle over each piece of parchment paper. Brush lightly with olive oil and season lightly with salt and pepper. Transfer the parchments to a baking sheet and bake 7 to 8 minutes, until the potatoes are lightly browned and crisp.
2. To serve: Reheat the broccoli puree and reserved florets if necessary and spoon into 4 warm soup plates. Arrange the potatoes in a circle around the puree. Place a broccoli floret in the center of each dish.

WHITE AND GREEN ASPARAGUS SALAD
WITH CITRUS LAVENDER VINAIGRETTE

Serves 4

A feast for the eyes as well as for the palate, this tart-sweet salad blends traditional Continental ingredients packed with flavor and health, and combines them with the unexpected citrus-flavor-packed pomelo. The resulting fusion is modern, elegant, and a perfect way to begin or even end a lavish meal.

1 bunch green asparagus (about 1 pound), trimmed and peeled
1 bunch white asparagus (about 1 pound), trimmed and peeled
1 large pomelo or grapefruit, halved
4 teaspoons extra virgin olive oil
Kosher salt and freshly ground black pepper
1 small head frisée, cored and torn into bite-size pieces
1 teaspoon dried lavender

1. Slice the asparagus on the bias into 1-inch-long pieces, 1/8 inch thick and place in a mixing bowl.
2. Section half of the pomelo and add it to the asparagus. Squeeze the juice from the other half (you should have 1/2 cup juice; if not, add enough lemon juice to equal 1/2 cup). Add the juice and olive oil to the asparagus. Season to taste with salt and pepper and toss well.
3. To serve: Center the frisée on 4 chilled plates. Arrange the asparagus salad over the frisée. Spoon any remaining dressing over the salads and sprinkle with lavender.

Eggplant Burgers
with Parmesan Cream Sauce

Serves 4

Imagine the most delectable, healthy version of the Israeli roasted eggplant dish baba ghanoush you've ever tasted, and then give it a distinctly modern twist: the result is an elegant, upscale cross between a classic salad and a traditional burger that can be served as part of a luxurious dinner or lunch menu. If you're in a time crunch, plan to roast the eggplant ahead of time; store the puree in an airtight container for up to a day prior to making the burgers. Make this dairy dish suitable for a meat menu by using egg substitute and a top-quality soy-based cheese, and omit the cream sauce.

2 pounds eggplant
Kosher salt and freshly ground black pepper
Extra virgin olive oil
2 garlic cloves, peeled and left whole
1/2 cup chopped red onion
2 eggs, lightly beaten
4 tablespoons finely grated Parmesan cheese
3 cups plus 2 tablespoons dry bread crumbs

1. Preheat oven to 400 degrees F. Season the eggplant with 2 teaspoons salt and pepper to taste. Transfer the eggplant, garlic, and red onion to a baking sheet and toss with 1 tablespoon olive oil. Roast for 35 to 40 minutes, until tender. Stir halfway through for even roasting. Turn the oven down to 250 degrees F.
2. Allow the eggplant to cool to room temperature and transfer to a food processor. Pulse to a coarse puree. Scrape the puree into a bowl and stir in the eggs, cheese, and 2 tablespoons bread crumbs.
3. Spread the remaining bread crumbs on a cookie sheet or large platter. Place a 1/3 cup scoop of eggplant puree in the crumbs and gently form into a patty 3/4 inches thick and 3 inches across. Repeat with remaining eggplant to form 8 patties.
4. Pour vegetable oil to the depth of 1/4 inch in an 8- to 10-inch skillet. Heat over medium-high heat until hot. Add 4 of the patties and fry 45 to 50 seconds per side, until golden brown and crisp. Transfer the patties to a baking sheet lined with parchment paper. Repeat with remaining patties. Transfer the patties to the oven to keep warm while you make the sauce.

Parmesan Cream Sauce

2 cups half-and-half
1/2 cup Parmesan cheese
1/4 teaspoon nutmeg, preferably freshly grated
4 teaspoons extra virgin olive oil
Kosher salt and freshly ground black pepper
8 basil leaves
12 grape tomatoes, halved

1. Combine the half-and-half, cheese, and nutmeg in a small sauce pan. Simmer over high heat for 1 minute. Add 2 teaspoons olive oil. Puree until smooth with a hand-held immersion blender*.
2. Boil the sauce over medium-high heat for 1 to 2 minutes, until it coats the back of a spoon. Season with salt and pepper.
3. Shred the basil leaves and toss in a small dish with remaining olive oil (this keeps the basil from turning black).
4. To serve: Scatter the basil over 2 plates. Arrange the burgers over the basil and spoon the sauce on top. Garnish with tomatoes halves and serve.

*Note: The sauce may also be pureed in a conventional standing blender, then poured back into the saucepan to continue cooking.

Vegetable Soup
(Potage aux Quatre Saisons)
Serves 4

Deeply comforting and incredibly delectable, this quick and simple *potage* bids farewell to long-simmering soups that take forever and a day to prepare. If you have the time, make this soup a day in advance in order to let the flavors meld; served hot or chilled, it will simply wow your guests. Or serve fresh from the pot and drizzle the greenest, highest quality extra virgin olive oil over the soup just before serving.

2 tablespoons plus 2 teaspoons extra virgin olive oil
2 cups finely diced sweet white onion
Kosher salt
1 cup finely chopped carrot
2 celery stalks, thinly sliced
1 cup chopped cabbage
2 small green zucchini, quartered lengthwise and thinly sliced
2 small golden zucchini, quartered lengthwise and thinly sliced
1 cup fresh shelled English peas
20 green beans, trimmed and sliced into 1/2-inch lengths
6 basil leaves, shredded
5 cups water or chicken stock
Freshly ground black pepper
Parmesan cheese

1. Heat 2 tablespoons oil in a 3- to 4-quart saucepan over medium heat until hot. Add the onion and a pinch of salt; sauté 3 to 4 minutes, until the onion is translucent; do not brown.
2. Add the carrots, celery, cabbage, and another pinch of salt and sauté 2 minutes.
3. Add the zucchini, peas, and green beans and sauté another 2 minutes.
4. Raise the heat, add water or stock, and bring to a boil. Reduce the heat to low and simmer, covered, 5 to 7 minutes, or until all the vegetables are tender.
5. Add the basil and remaining olive oil. Season with salt and pepper. Sprinkle with Parmesan for serving.

Winter Salad
with Porcini Mushrooms
Serves 4

In the cool of the fall and winter, food markets from coast to coast abound with an earthy yet sophisticated array of dazzling flavors and textures so stunning that it's hard to believe that the growing season, for many of us, is ending. There is no better way to take advantage of this sumptuous bounty than by creating this elegant winter salad, which can function either as an appetizer or after-dinner salad course.

8 ounces fresh porcini mushrooms, rinsed and patted dry
2 teaspoons black truffle oil
2 teaspoons lemon juice
12 Belgian endive leaves, cored and julienned
4 cups loosely packed tiny mesclun greens
4 teaspoons extra virgin olive oil
Kosher salt and freshly ground black pepper
2 tablespoons aged balsamic vinegar
One 2- inch chunk Parmesan cheese

1. Thinly slice the porcini mushrooms and spread them in the center of 4 plates. Sprinkle the mushrooms with the truffle oil and 1 teaspoon lemon juice.
2. Toss the endive and greens with the olive oil and remaining lemon juice. Season with salt and black pepper.
3. Mound the greens on top of the mushrooms. Drizzle with balsamic vinegar. Shave the Parmesan over the greens and serve.

POLENTA CROSTINI
WITH ZUCCHINI, BRIE, AND TOMATO OLIVE VINAIGRETTE

Serves 4

This deliciously healthy twist on traditional crostini marries the ages-old Mediterranean flavors of tomatoes and olives with the summery flavors of corn and zucchini. Clean-tasting yet richly fulfilling, it's simply wonderful served alongside a salad of the freshest tossed greens you can find, or as an appetizer or tapas for a casual dinner party.

For the crostini:
4 1/2 cups water
2 teaspoons butter
1/4 teaspoon kosher salt
1 1/2 cups polenta (not instant)
1/2 teaspoon extra virgin olive oil

1. Combine the water, butter, and salt in a 2- to 3-quart sauce pan. Bring to a boil over high heat.
2. Slowly whisk in the polenta. Reduce the heat to medium-low and simmer, stirring occasionally, for 25 to 30 minutes, until the polenta is thick and smooth and pulls away from the sides of the pan.
3. Cut two 15 x 15-inch sheets of parchment or wax paper. Brush each piece with oil. Spread the polenta evenly over the parchment and place the second piece on top, oiled side down. With a rolling pin, roll the polenta into a 1/4-inch-thick rectangle. Set aside to cool until firm.

For the vinaigrette:
1 cup grape tomatoes
1/2 cup kalamata olives, pitted and halved lengthwise
1 medium shallot, peeled and finely chopped
1 teaspoon sherry vinegar
1 teaspoon extra virgin olive oil
Kosher salt and freshly ground black pepper

Slice 3/4 cup of the tomatoes in half and place in a bowl. Pass the remaining tomatoes through a food mill into the bowl. Add the olives, shallot, vinegar, and oil. Season with salt and pepper and toss to combine.

To assemble and bake the crostini:
1 medium zucchini (about 8 ounces), cut into eight 1/4-inch-thick rounds
Extra virgin olive oil
Kosher salt
4 ounces Brie, rind removed, cut into 8 slices
1/2 cup finely grated Parmesan cheese

1. Preheat the oven to 450 degrees F. Brush both sides of the zucchini with oil and sprinkle with salt.
2. Place the zucchini on a preheated grill pan or heavy, wide skillet over medium heat. Cook the zucchini undisturbed for 2 to 3 minutes per side, until tender and pocked in spots.
3. With a cookie cutter, cut out sixteen 2-inch rounds of polenta and transfer 8 polenta rounds to a baking sheet. Top each round with 1 slice each of zucchini and Brie. Place the remaining rounds on top to make sandwiches. Brush the tops with oil and sprinkle with Parmesan. Bake for 8 minutes, until the Parmesan is browned and crisp.
4. To serve: Place 2 polenta sandwiches on each of 4 plates. Spoon 1/4 of the vinaigrette over each and serve immediately.

Fresh Herbed Couscous with Feta and Orange

Serves 4

Sweet, salty, savory, crunchy, brightly colored, and incredibly healthy: what could possibly be more refreshing and delicious than this couscous salad redolent of herbs, lemon, and orange? Dressed on fresh mesclun greens and presented on magnificent plates, this simple-to-prepare salad will win raves at the most luxurious dinner party or the most romantic evening à deux.

1 cup instant couscous
1 cup plus 1 tablespoon boiling water
1 teaspoon extra virgin olive oil
1/2 teaspoon kosher salt

For the dressing:
2 seedless oranges
1/2 cup, firmly packed mixed fresh herb leaves, such as mint, parsley, dill, and thyme, finely chopped
1 tablespoon lemon juice
4 tablespoons plus 1/4 teaspoon extra virgin olive oil
6 ounces feta cheese
1/4 cup walnuts, lightly toasted and coarsely chopped
Kosher salt and freshly ground black pepper
2 small Jerusalem artichokes or the hearts of 2 baby artichokes, trimmed and shaved paper thin
1 cup lightly packed mesclun greens
1/4 teaspoon extra virgin olive oil

1. Place the couscous, olive oil, and salt in a small bowl. Stir in the boiling water. Cover the bowl and set aside for 10 minutes until all the liquid has been absorbed and the couscous is tender.
2. Make the dressing: Grate the zest of 1 orange with a rasp into a mixing bowl. Add the chopped herbs, lemon juice, and olive oil.
3. Peel the oranges of all rind and pith, and slice between the membranes to form neat wedges. Reserve 8 wedges for garnish and cut the remainder crosswise into 1/2-inch pieces.
4. Toss the couscous, orange pieces, feta cheese, and walnuts with the dressing. Season with salt and pepper.
5. To serve: Spoon the couscous onto the center of 4 plates. Surround the couscous with mesclun. Top the couscous with shaved artichoke and reserved orange wedges. Drizzle olive oil over the couscous and serve.

Potato Gallettes with Fresh Ricotta, Black Olives, and Basil

Serves 4

A healthy kosher adaptation of the traditional *galette de pommes de terres*, a dish beloved by the Roman emperors, these scrumptious potato cakes blend the earthy flavors of Provence and Italy. If fresh basil is not available, consider using fresh rosemary, which is also very friendly with potatoes and black olives.

2 pounds Yukon gold potatoes, peeled and coarsely grated Kosher salt and freshly ground black pepper
4 tablespoons plus 2 teaspoons extra virgin olive oil
8 tablespoons fresh ricotta cheese
2 tablespoons chopped black olives
Fleur de sel or kosher salt
4 teaspoons chopped basil flowers
2 teaspoons aged balsamic vinegar (at least 12 years old)

1. In a bowl combine the grated potatoes and 1/2 teaspoon salt. Allow the mixture to sit for 5 minutes, then squeeze dry. Stir in 4 tablespoons olive oil and season with pepper.
2. Press the potatoes into 4 round cakes each 4 inches across.
3. Heat a wide nonstick skillet over medium heat until hot. Add the gallettes to the pan. Lower the heat and cook for 20 minutes, turning every 5 minutes until the gallettes are golden brown and crisp.
4. To serve, transfer the pancakes to plates and top each with 2 tablespoons ricotta. Sprinkle with fleur de sel.
5. Scatter the chopped olives and basil flowers over and around the galletes. Drizzle each plate with 1/2 teaspoon extra virgin olive oil and several drops of aged balsamic vinegar.

STUFFED CABBAGE
WITH CHANTERELLES, RICOTTA, AND SALSA CRUDA

Serves 4

This surprisingly healthy, modern take on traditional stuffed cabbage and tomato sauce. Redolent of cumin, garlic, and fresh tomatoes, this tasty dish is low in fat, long on flavor, and truly stunning in presentation.

4 Savoy cabbage leaves 5 to 6 inches wide, thick central rib removed
Kosher salt
2 tablespoons extra virgin olive oil
2 garlic cloves, unpeeled and lightly crushed with the side of a knife
8 ounces chanterelle mushrooms, rinsed and patted dry
1 tablespoon finely chopped parsley
1/2 cup fresh ricotta cheese
2 tablespoons finely grated Parmesan cheese
2 small pinches ground cumin
2 tablespoons butter
Extra virgin olive oil

1. Preheat the oven to 400 degrees F. Blanch the cabbage leaves in lightly salted boiling water for 2 to 3 minutes, until wilted. Transfer the cabbage to a bowl of ice water until cold, and drain well on several layers of paper towel.

2. Heat the olive oil in a wide sauté pan over medium-high heat until hot. Add the garlic and sauté 1 minute. Add the mushrooms and a pinch of salt. Sauté 2 minutes, until the mushrooms give up most of their liquid. Add the parsley and 2 tablespoons water. Simmer 3 minutes, until the mushrooms are tender. Transfer the mushrooms and their juices to a bowl. Discard the garlic. Stir in ricotta, Parmesan, cumin, and 1/4 teaspoon salt.

3. Lay a cabbage leaf on a clean surface and cut out the base of the rib if it is large. Place a mound of filling in the bottom third of the leaf and fold up the bottom to cover it. Fold the sides of the leaf into the center, then roll up the leaf to form a neat package. Fill the remaining cabbage leaves in the same manner.

4. Melt the butter in a wide ovenproof skillet over medium heat. Place the cabbage rolls seam side down in the skillet. Baste the tops of the cabbage with butter and sprinkle with 1 teaspoon Parmesan. Transfer the skillet to the oven and bake for 4 to 5 minutes, until heated through.

5. To serve: Divide the salsa between 4 soup plates. Transfer the cabbage rolls to a cutting board and slice on the bias in half. Place 1/2 roll in the center of each plate, and lean the other half against the first. Drizzle several drops of your best extra virgin olive oil around the sauce and serve.

Salsa Cruda

This salsa cruda—or "raw" sauce—benefits from using the freshest, most seasonal tomatoes you can find. Any leftover salsa can be stored in an airtight jar in the refrigerator for up to 3 days; spoon it over everything from lightly steamed vegetables to fresh fish or chicken.

4 medium yellow tomatoes, coarsely chopped
2 tablespoons extra virgin olive oil
Kosher salt and freshly ground black pepper

In a blender puree the tomatoes with oil until smooth. Pass the puree through a fine sieve into a bowl and season with salt and pepper.

VEGETABLE BROTH
WITH ARTICHOKE CROUTONS

Serves 4

This luxurious yet rustic dish is tasty but not filling, a magnificent way to begin a meal, with sumptuous textures, colors, and flavors.

2 teaspoons extra virgin olive oil
2 garlic cloves, unpeeled and lightly bruised with the side of a knife
2 globe artichoke hearts, pared and thinly sliced
8 cups vegetable stock
1/2 cup fresh peas
4 tablespoons thinly sliced carrot
2 scallions, trimmed and thinly sliced
8 slices baguette, 1/4 inch thick on the diagonal
8 tablespoons fromage blanc or cream cheese
Kosher salt and freshly ground black pepper
4 tablespoons white wine vinegar
8 small kosher chicken eggs
Fleur de sel or kosher salt
2 teaspoons finely chopped parsley

1. Light the broiler. Heat the oil in a wide nonstick skillet over high heat until hot. Add the garlic and artichokes. Sauté 2 to 3 minutes until the artichokes are golden brown. Discard the garlic. Transfer the artichokes to a small dish.

2. Combine the vegetable stock, peas, carrots, and scallions in a saucepan and simmer over medium heat until the vegetables are tender, 3 to 4 minutes.

3. Spread each baguette slice with 1 tablespoon fromage blanc or cream cheese. Transfer to a baking sheet and broil 6 inches from the heat for 3 to 4 minutes, until lightly browned. Remove the croutons from the broiler and top each with sliced artichoke.

4. Combine 2 cups water and 2 tablespoons vinegar in a small sauce pan and bring to a simmer over medium heat.

5. Crack an egg into a teacup. Gently pour the egg into the simmering water and poach 1 minute. Using a slotted spoon, place the egg on top of a crouton. Repeat with the remaining eggs.

6. To serve: Ladle the broth and vegetables into warm soup plates. Arrange the eggs and croutons on top of the broth. Sprinkle each crouton lightly with fleur de sel and chopped parsley.

PIZZA AND PASTA

The Billionaire's Classic Red Sauce

Makes enough sauce for four 11-inch thin-crusted pizzas or 1 pound pasta

Audrey Hepburn had her famed little black dress; Jean Seberg had her striped T-shirt; and Chanel her tiny bouclé jacket. Every icon has a signature, and in the case of the kosher billionaire in the kitchen, she has her classic red sauce, which can go from pizza to pasta and beyond in minutes. Simple, delicious, and light, it can be prepared in minutes.

One 14-ounce can organic plum tomatoes with juice
1/4 teaspoon kosher salt
1/4 teaspoon dried oregano
Freshly ground black pepper
1 small garlic clove, peeled and crushed
6 large basil leaves

Combine all ingredients in a food processor and pulse to form a coarse puree with flecks of basil.

The Billionaire's Perfect Pizza Dough

Makes four 11-inch thin-crusted pizzas

This simple, quick all-purpose pizza dough recipe will forever change your mind about preparing your own dough: make it in bulk, freeze it, and you'll have the base for any pizza, calzone, or tart ready and available in your own kitchen.

1 3/4 cups lukewarm water
2 tablespoons olive oil
1 packet dry active yeast
4 cups all-purpose flour
1 teaspoon kosher salt

1. Mix water and olive oil, sprinkle in the yeast, and set aside until the yeast is creamy and begins to bubble, about 10 minutes.
2. Place the flour and salt in a large bowl and stir to combine. Stir in the yeast mixture and mix with a wooden spoon until the dough comes together in a shaggy mass. Transfer the dough to a clean surface and knead 10 minutes, until smooth and elastic. The dough will be slightly tacky.
3. Divide the dough into 4 equal pieces and form each piece into a ball.
4. Transfer the balls of dough to a lightly greased baking sheet and cover loosely with plastic wrap. Place the baking sheet in a draft-free place and let rise 1 to 2 hours, until doubled in volume.
5. Press down on each ball of dough to deflate it, reshape into rounds, and let rise again until doubled in volume.
6. The dough is ready to bake or can be refrigerated for up to 24 hours or frozen for 3 months.

Greek Pizza

One 11-inch pizza

Perfect as a casual snack, or sliced into squares and served as an hors d'oeuvre at the most elegant dinner party, this traditional Greek pizza is kicked up a notch with the addition of top quality Greek feta cheese. *'Opa!*

1 tablespoon cornmeal
1/4 recipe Billionaire's Perfect Pizza Dough (page 185)
1/4 recipe Billionaire's Classic Red Sauce (page 185)
3 ounces Greek feta cheese
6 kalamata olives, pitted and halved
1 fresh plum tomato, seeded and diced

1. Place a pizza stone on a rack in the upper third of the oven and preheat the oven to 500 degrees F for 30 minutes.
2. Dust a baker's peel or cookie sheet with cornmeal.
3. Roll out the dough into an 11-inch round. Transfer the dough to the peel.
4. Spread the sauce over the dough with the back of a spoon, leaving a 1/2-inch border.
5. Crumble the feta over the red sauce, dot with olives, and scatter with tomato.
6. Transfer the pizza to the stone and bake for 8 minutes, until the dough is browned and crisp. Transfer the pizza to a platter and serve.

Porcini Pizza with Taleggio and Cream

One 11-inch pizza

Here the northern Italian flavors of silky, pungent Taleggio, earthy porcini, and woodsy black truffles combine for a wildly indulgent—yet healthy—gourmet pizza that will become a favorite of all your guests. If fresh porcini are not available, substitute cremini or baby portabellas.

1 tablespoon cornmeal
1/4 recipe Billionaire's Perfect Pizza Dough (page 185)
3 ounces fresh porcini mushrooms, thinly sliced
1 garlic clove, lightly crushed
2/3 cup heavy cream
2 1/2 ounces Taleggio cheese, thinly sliced
2 teaspoons chopped parsley
Black truffle oil

1. Place a pizza stone on a rack in the upper third of the oven and preheat the oven to 500 degrees F for 30 minutes.
2. Dust a baker's peel or cookie sheet with cornmeal. Roll out the dough into an 11-inch round. Transfer the dough to the peel.
3. Heat the olive oil in an 8- to 10-inch skillet over medium heat until hot. Add the mushrooms and garlic and sauté 3 to 4 minutes, until golden brown.
4. Add the cream and cheese, raise the heat to medium-high, and boil for 1 minute, until thickened.
5. Transfer the dough onto the pizza stone and carefully spread with the mushroom cream. Bake 8 minutes, until the dough is browned and crisp. Transfer the pizza to a platter, sprinkle with parsley, drizzle with truffle oil, and serve.

182

Pizza Vegano
(Vegan Tofu Pizza)

Gone are the days when vegan pizza meant stodgy, stiff, and heavy; my chefworthy version will forever change your mind! Here, the addition of red wine vinegar and rosemary oil lends a distinctly parmigiana-like taste to the tofu cheese, which can also be enjoyed on bruschetta, flatbread, or alongside any meat dish.

Pizza

1 tablespoon cornmeal
1/4 recipe Billionaire's Perfect Pizza Dough (page 185)
1 tablespoon plus 2 teaspoons rosemary oil (recipe below)
2 large ripe plum tomatoes, sliced into 1/4-inch-thick rounds
Kosher salt
1/2 teaspoon crushed red pepper flakes
1 teaspoon aged balsamic vinegar or to taste
1 tablespoon chopped basil

1. Place a pizza stone on a rack in the upper third of the oven and preheat the oven to 500 degrees F for 30 minutes.
2. Dust a baker's peel or cookie sheet with cornmeal. Roll out the dough into an 11-inch round. Transfer the dough to the peel and drizzle with 1 tablespoon rosemary oil.
3. Lay the tomatoes on the dough. Season with salt and crushed red pepper. Top with the tofu cheese mixture (recipe below).
4. Slide the pizza onto the stone and bake for 8 minutes, until the tofu cheese is golden and the tomatoes are soft and juicy. Remove the pizza to a platter, drizzle with remaining 2 teaspoons rosemary oil and aged balsamic vinegar. Sprinkle with basil and serve.

Tofu Cheese

4 ounces extra-firm tofu
3 tablespoons rosemary oil (recipe below)
1/4 teaspoon kosher salt
1 teaspoon red wine vinegar

Combine all the ingredients in a bowl and mash to the consistency of ricotta cheese.

Rosemary Oil

Use any leftover oil for vinaigrette, drizzling over steamed vegetables, or for brushing on fish or meat before grilling.

1/2 cup extra virgin olive oil
One 2-inch rosemary sprig
2 garlic cloves, peeled and halved

Combine the ingredients in a small saucepan. Cook at a gentle simmer over low heat for 15 minutes, until the garlic is golden. Remove the pan from the heat and cool. Strain and it is ready to use.

Vegetable Pizza
with Three Cheeses

One 11-inch pizza

This luscious pizza will satisfy the most finicky pizza lover's wildest craving. A veritable salad on a pizza, it is rich yet light, flavorful yet healthy. Enjoy it anytime, but especially when it's zucchini season!

1 tablespoon cornmeal
1 teaspoon extra virgin olive oil
1/4 recipe Billionaire's Perfect Pizza Dough (page 185)
1/2 cup thinly sliced red onion
1/2 bell pepper diced
3 leaves Belgian endive, thinly sliced
1/2 medium zucchini, green part only, diced
3 thin slices eggplant, from a medium eggplant
1/4 cup Billionaire's Classic Red Sauce (page 185)
2 ounces ricotta cheese
1 ounce fresh mozzarella cheese, thinly sliced
2 tablespoons finely grated Parmesan cheese

1. Place a pizza stone on a rack in the upper third of the oven and preheat the oven to 500 degrees F for 30 minutes.
2. Dust a baker's peel or a cookie sheet with cornmeal. Roll out the dough into an 11-inch round. Transfer the dough to the peel.
3. Heat olive oil in an 8- to 10-inch nonstick skillet over high heat. Add the vegetables and sauté 3 to 4 minutes, until lightly browned. Reduce the heat to low and cook 2 to 3 minutes, until the vegetables are soft and juicy.
4. Spread the red sauce over the dough, leaving a 1/2-inch border. Dot with ricotta and top with mozzarella. Spread the vegetables over the top and sprinkle with Parmesan. Bake 8 minutes, until the cheese is bubbling and the crust is golden brown and crisp.

Parmesan Crème Brûlée

Serves 6

1 egg
4 teaspoons finely grated Parmesan cheese
1/2 cup heavy cream
4 scrapes of fresh nutmeg
1/2 teaspoon salt

1. Preheat the oven to 275 degrees F. In a bowl, whisk the ingredients until well combined. Spoon the custard into six 2-ounce ramekins.
2. Transfer the ramekins to a roasting pan and place on the middle shelf of the oven. Gently pour enough boiling water around the ramekins to come halfway up the sides. Bake for 40 minutes until set. Place the ramekins 2 inches from the broiler for 1 minute, until lightly browned. Serve immediately with ravioli.

Fresh Ricotta and Spinach Ravioli
with Parmesan Crème Brûlée

Serves 6

These opulent, tasty homemade ravioli are festive and elegant, a kosher billionaire favorite for celebrations.

For the ravioli:
8 ounces all-purpose flour
6 egg yolks
1 whole egg
1 1/2 tablespoons olive oil
1 tablespoon milk

Combine all the ingredients in a food processor and pulse to combine. Turn out onto a clean surface and knead for 1 minute until smooth. Wrap in plastic wrap until ready to use. Dough can be refrigerated for 3 days or frozen for 1 month.

For the filling:
1 teaspoon extra virgin olive oil
One 2-inch rosemary sprig
1 garlic clove, unpeeled and lightly crushed
5 ounces prewashed baby spinach
1 cup fresh ricotta cheese
1/2 cup finely grated Parmesan cheese
Pinch kosher salt
Freshly ground black pepper

1. Heat the oil in a 12- to 14-inch nonstick skillet over medium-high heat until hot. Add the rosemary, garlic, and spinach and sauté, stirring frequently, until the spinach is dry. Discard the garlic and rosemary.

2. Transfer the spinach to a food processor and pulse until finely chopped. Add the ricotta and Parmesan, and season with salt and black pepper. Pulse until the mixture is combined and transfer to a bowl.

3. Divide the ravioli dough into 4 equal pieces and form each piece into a circle. Work with one piece at a time, keeping the remaining dough under plastic wrap. Fold the circle into thirds and roll the narrow end through the widest setting on your pasta roller. Repeat this 4 to 5 times. Now thin the dough by tightening the rollers, one notch at a time, passing the dough once through each setting, up to number 6.

4. Place rounded teaspoons of filling every 2 inches lengthwise along one half of the dough, leaving a 1/2-inch border. With a damp pastry brush, moisten the areas between each mound of filling. Fold the other half over to meet the edge and gently press around each mound of filling to seal. Cut the ravioli and set aside on a clean towel to dry. Do not let them touch or they could stick together. Continue to roll, fill, and seal the remaining pieces of dough.

5. Boil the ravioli for 2 to 3 minutes, until cooked through. Drain and transfer to warm serving plates.

To serve:
6 tablespoons butter
1 tablespoon chopped fresh sage

Heat the butter and sage together in a small skillet until foamy. Pour the sauce over the raviolis and serve accompanied by Parmesan Crème Brûlée (recipe previous page).

185

Orzotto with Asparagus

This healthy orzotto (like risotto, but based on barley instead of rice) is dense, delicious, and absolutely decadent. Packed with all the minerals that whole grains have to offer and reminiscent of the richest traditional risotto you've had anywhere this side of Venice, it is sure to become a favorite.

1 cup coarse, medium, or fine pearl barley
1/2 cup half-and-half
12 stalks green asparagus
12 stalks white asparagus
1 tablespoon butter
1 tablespoon olive oil
2 heaping tablespoons finely chopped onion
1/2 cup dry white wine
7 cups vegetable stock (see following)
4 tablespoons heavy cream
4 tablespoons grated Parmesan cheese plus additional shavings for serving
2 teaspoons finely chopped parsley

1. Combine the barley, half-and-half, and 1/2 cup water in a bowl and soak for 1 hour.
2. Cut the tips from the asparagus stalks and reserve. Cut off the bottom 1 inch from each stalk and reserve for use in the vegetable stock (recipe below). Slice the stalks crosswise into 1/8-inch-thick rounds.
3. Heat 1/2 tablespoon butter and the oil in a small saucepan over medium heat until hot. Add the onion and sliced asparagus stalks, sauté for 2 to 3 minutes, until the vegetables soften.
4. Stir in the barley and sauté 1 minute. Add the wine and simmer for 30 seconds.
5. Add the stock, raise the heat, and bring to a boil. Reduce the heat and simmer, uncovered, for 20 minutes or until the barley is tender and most of the liquid is absorbed.
6. Add the reserved asparagus tips and simmer 1 minute.
7. Stir in the heavy cream, Parmesan, parsley, and remaining butter. Allow the risotto to sit for 2 minutes before serving to allow the barley to absorb some of the cream.
8. Serve in warm soup plates garnished with Parmesan shavings.

Vegetable Stock

10 cups water
1 medium onion
4 celery stalks, halved
2 parsley sprigs
2 carrots, peeled and halved
1 bay leaf
1 garlic clove, peeled and halved
1 small zucchini, halved lengthwise
Reserved ends of asparagus from orzotto recipe above, or bottom 2 inches from the stalks of 1 bunch asparagus
1 tablespoon kosher salt

Combine all of the ingredients in a pot and simmer, uncovered, over medium-low heat for 1 hour. Drain and discard the solids. Any leftover may be frozen for 3 months.

Garganelle Pasta with Chicken Livers, Caramelized Onion, and Marsala

Serves 4

Succulent and rich, this very traditional ragù-style dish features one of our favorite pasta shapes—garganelle, toothsome little twists that are a perfect vehicle for denser meat-based sauces. Prepare this when the temperature dips a bit; serve it to your sweetheart in front of a roaring fire, and watch the sparks fly!

4 tablespoons extra virgin olive oil
2/3 cup thinly sliced onion
2 garlic cloves, peeled and finely chopped
6 tablespoons finely diced carrot
2 tablespoons finely diced celery
4 teaspoons coarsely chopped Italian parsley
8 ounces chicken livers, cleaned and coarsely chopped
Kosher salt and freshly ground black pepper
2/3 cup marsala wine
2/3 cup vegetable stock
One 2-inch rosemary sprig
8 ounces garganelli pasta

1. Heat the olive oil over high heat in a 10- to 12-inch skillet until hot. Add the vegetables and parsley and sauté 1 minute. Stir in the livers and sauté 2 to 3 minutes. Season with salt and pepper.
2. Add the marsala but do not stir it in. Turn off the heat under the pan and, preferably with a long kitchen match, flame the pan. When the flame subsides, return the pan to medium heat.
3. Add the vegetable stock. Reduce the heat and simmer 2 to 3 minutes, until the liquid is reduced slightly.
4. Add the rosemary, simmer 1 minute longer, and remove the pan from the heat. Discard the rosemary.
5. Cook the pasta until al dente. Reheat the sauce. Drain the pasta and add to the sauce toss to combine. Spoon the pasta into 2 warm pasta plates, top with caramelized onions (below), and serve.

Caramelized Onions

2 teaspoons extra virgin olive oil
1 red onion, sliced into 1/4-inch-thick crescents from root to stem
2 teaspoons aged balsamic vinegar
Kosher salt and freshly ground black pepper

Heat the oil in a medium skillet over high heat until hot. Add the onions and sauté, stirring the onions and shaking the pan for 2 to 3 minutes, until they are lightly and evenly browned. Transfer the onions to a small dish and stir in balsamic vinegar. Season with salt and pepper.

Spaghetti Pomodoro

Serves 4

Everyone loves tradition, and when the best-quality plum tomatoes are available, this dish is the one to prepare. Look for San Marzano tomatoes, which are sweeter and pulpier than standard plum tomatoes, and better suited to saucy endeavors.

One 14-ounce can peeled plum tomatoes
1/4 cup extra virgin olive oil
1 bay leaf
2 garlic cloves, peeled and finely chopped
1/2 cup coarsely chopped onions
1/4 cup coarsely chopped basil leaves, loosely packed
1/4 teaspoon sugar
Kosher salt and freshly ground black pepper
8 ounces spaghetti
Whole basil leaves for garnish
Freshly grated Parmesan cheese for serving

1. Pour the tomatoes and their liquid into a bowl and crush with your fingers or mash with a fork to a coarse puree.
2. Combine the olive oil, bay leaf, garlic, onions, and basil in a heavy, 2- to 3-quart saucepan. Cook over high heat, stirring occasionally, for 3 to 4 minutes, until the onion has softened.
3. Add the tomatoes, 1/4 cup water, and sugar, and season with salt and pepper. Bring the sauce to a boil and remove the bay leaf. Reduce the heat and simmer the sauce uncovered for 10 minutes, until the oil comes to the surface and the sauce has thickened.
4. Boil the spaghetti in salted water for 8 to 10 minutes, until al dente.
5. Drain the pasta and reserve 2 tablespoons of the cooking liquid. Combine the pasta, sauce, and cooking water and simmer 1 to 2 minutes to finish the spaghetti. Serve in warm pasta plates garnished with basil leaves and accompanied by freshly grated Parmesan cheese if desired.

FISH

OVEN-ROASTED RED SNAPPER
WITH VEGETABLES AND SALT-BAKED SHALLOTS

Serves 4

This magnificent dish sings of sultry nights on the Mediterranean, and meals wildly fresh, healthy, and decadent, reminiscent of our favorite meals enjoyed aboard the *Christina O*. The fish is brought whole to the table on a bed of colorful vegetables, alongside buttery-tender, incredibly sweet shallots. A celebratory dish that defines elegance.

1/4 cup plus 1 tablespoon extra virgin olive oil
1 large red onion, halved lengthwise and sliced into 1/4-inch thick crescents
    (about 2 cups)
4 celery stalks, halved lengthwise and cut across into 1-inch pieces
2 medium carrots, halved lengthwise, and sliced across into 1-inch pieces
1 whole red snapper (about 2 1/2 pounds), cleaned, fins removed
6 branches mixed fresh herbs, such as marjoram, thyme, and rosemary
1 cup loosely packed basil leaves
Kosher salt and freshly ground black pepper
2 garlic cloves, peeled and halved
1 pound fingerling potatoes, scrubbed and halved lengthwise
1/2 cup black pitted olives (such as kalamata)
1 cup grape tomatoes
2 medium zucchini (about 1 pound), quartered lengthwise and sliced to
    make 3-inch sticks
3/4 cup any dry kosher white wine

1. Preheat the oven to 400 degrees F. Brush a roasting pan with 1 tablespoon olive oil. Spread the onions, celery, and carrots in the pan.
2. Rinse the fish under cold running water and dry thoroughly with paper towel. Season the inside of the fish with 1/2 teaspoon salt and stuff with herbs, 1/2 of the basil leaves, and 1/2 of the garlic. Lay the fish on top on the vegetables.
3. Simmer the potatoes in lightly salted water to cover for 15 minutes or until slightly tender but still firm. Drain the potatoes and transfer them to the roasting pan. Scatter the olives and the remaining basil leaves and garlic around the fish.
4. Toss the tomatoes and zucchini with 1/4 cup olive oil and add to the pan.
5. Sprinkle 1 teaspoon salt over the fish and vegetables, and season with freshly ground black pepper.
6. Transfer the pan to a rack in the middle of the oven for 20 minutes. Pour wine over and around the fish and roast for 15 minutes more for a total of 35 minutes, or until the fish flakes. Meanwhile, prepare the Salt-Baked Shallots.
7. Fillet the fish and divide it among 4 warm soup plates. Spoon the vegetables and pan juices over and around the fish, garnish with the Salt-Baked Shallots, and serve.

Salt-Baked Shallots

6 medium shallots
1 teaspoon extra virgin olive oil
2 tarragon sprigs
2 cups fleur de sel or other high-quality coarse-grained sea salt

1. Gently peel the outer tough skin from the shallots and trim off the root end.
2. Place 1 cup fleur de sel in a 6-inch ovenproof skillet, lay the shallots on top, and drizzle with olive oil. Lay the sprigs of tarragon over the shallots and cover completely with the remaining fleur de sel. Transfer the skillet to the oven and roast for 30 minutes or until tender when pierced with a thin knife.
3. Remove the shallots from the salt and transfer to a plate to cool. Again, peel off the outer skin, then serve whole along with the fish and vegetables.

189

Pan-Seared Ahi Tuna Fillet Scottato with Red Onion Marmalade and Herb Salad

Layered with baby greens and herbs, crunchy flavorful red onion, and tender tuna, this dish sings of the Amalfi coast, where the fish has been caught that day, all the people are beautiful, and it's oh so glorious to be a healthy kosher billionaire!

Red Onion Marmalade

6 tablespoons *mild honey*
4 teaspoons coarse-grained Dijon mustard
4 teaspoons aged balsamic vinegar
4 large red onions, thinly sliced (about 4 cups)
4 teaspoons Rapadura (natural evaporated cane juice crystals) or brown
    sugar
2 teaspoons kosher salt
4 tablespoons Armagnac or other good brandy
4 tablespoons water

Combine all ingredients in a small saucepan over low heat for 30 to 40 minutes, until the onions begin to caramelize. Add the brandy and water. Simmer 2 to 3 minutes until thickened. Serve hot or at room temperature.

Herb Salad

2 cups sunflower sprouts
1 cup mesclun greens
6 tablespoons tiny basil leaves and flowers
4 tablespoons tiny mint leaves, stems removed
4 tablespoons parsley leaves, stems removed
2 teaspoons extra virgin olive oil
2 fennel bulbs, trimmed and shaved on a mandoline or very thinly sliced
Kosher salt and freshly ground black pepper

For the vinaigrette:
1 teaspoon minced pickled ginger
2 teaspoons lemon juice
4 teaspoons hazelnut oil
1 garlic clove, halved
1/2 teaspoon kosher salt

1. Rub the inside of a small bowl with the garlic half. Add the vinaigrette ingredients and mix to combine.
2. In a separate bowl toss the sprouts, salad greens, and herbs with oil. Season with salt and black pepper. Reserve the shaved fennel in a separate dish.

For the tuna:
Four 6-ounce center-cut tuna steaks 1 inch thick
Kosher salt and freshly ground black pepper
2 teaspoons olive oil

Pat the tuna dry and season on both sides with salt and pepper. Heat the oil in a nonstick skillet over medium-high heat until hot. Add the tuna steaks and sear for 30 seconds on each side or until medium rare.

To serve: Slice each piece of tuna crosswise in half. Spoon the red onion marmalade onto each plate, lay one piece of tuna on the marmalade, and stand the other piece against it. Top the tuna with shaved fennel and drizzle with vinaigrette. Place a mound of herb salad next to the tuna and serve.

GRILLED MARINATED SALMON
WITH BEET CARPACCIO AND BELL PEPPER PUREE

Fresh salmon is not only delicious and brilliantly colorful: it is positively packed with heart-healthy omega-3 fatty acids. Paired with a sweet beet carpaccio and full-bodied yet light bell pepper puree, this creation has become a favorite among all my guests, and is as healthy as it is succulent.

Bell Pepper Puree

1 large yellow bell pepper, cored, quartered lengthwise, and sliced
    into 1-inch chunks
1 medium Yukon Gold potato, about 8 ounces, peeled and coarsely chopped
1 large garlic clove, peeled and halved
1 tablespoon olive oil
1 sprig marjoram
1/2 teaspoon kosher salt and freshly ground black pepper

1. Combine the pepper, potato, garlic, oil, marjoram, and salt in a small saucepan. Cover with 2 cups cold water and season with black pepper.
2. Bring to a boil over a high heat, reduce to a simmer, uncovered, until the potatoes crush easily when pressed against the side of the pan, about 15 minutes. Transfer to a blender and puree until smooth.

Beet Carpaccio

4 baby golden beets, trimmed, peeled, and shaved paper thin
2 teaspoons olive oil
Kosher salt and freshly ground black pepper

Toss the beets with oil. Season with a pinch of salt and pepper, and then refrigerate until ready to serve.

Grilled Marinated Salmon

4 pieces center-cut salmon fillet with skin (about 6 ounces each)
Kosher salt and freshly ground black pepper
1/2 teaspoon fennel seed
1/2 teaspoon coriander seeds, lightly crushed
4 juniper berries, lightly crushed
1/4 teaspoon ground ginger
2 teaspoons lemon juice
1 tablespoon chopped fennel fronds or chives for garnish

1. Preheat the oven to 400 degrees F. Season the salmon with salt and pepper. Combine the remaining ingredients in a small bowl and transfer to a platter.

2. Place the salmon flesh side down on the mixture and refrigerate for 30 minutes.
3. Heat an ovenproof nonstick pan over high heat until hot. Place the salmon skin side down in the pan and cook 2 minutes, until the skin is crisp. Turn the fish over and place the pan in the oven. Roast for 5 minutes. Remove the pan from the oven.

To serve:
4 black olives, halved and pitted
1 tablespoon chives, finely chopped

Place 1/3 cup bell pepper puree on the center of a plate. Dot the puree with olives. Place the salmon over the puree and top with beet carpaccio. Sprinkle with chopped fennel or chives and serve.

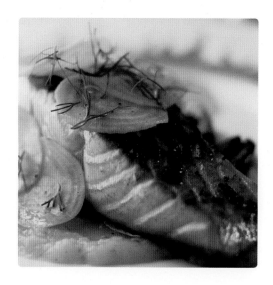

Halibut Livornese
with Spinach Mashed Potatoes

Nestled on the sun-drenched western coast of Italy, south of Milan and north of the Amalfi coast, lies the ancient port city of Livorno, where merchants of nearly every conceivable background brought with them the healthful flavors of their home countries. In this lusciously flavorful dish, firm, sweet, white-fleshed halibut comes together with Mediterranean olives, capers, basil, and tomato and is served with a healthy mash of emerald-green spinach and potatoes for a result that will leave you hearing the sound of the Livornese buoys as if they were only a few feet away.

4 tablespoons olive oil
8 anchovy fillets packed in oil, drained and finely chopped
1 cup dry white wine
2 1/2 cups grape tomatoes
2 tablespoons capers, packed in vinegar, drained
2 shallots, finely chopped
1/2 cup firmly packed shredded basil leaves
16 kalamata olives, pitted and halved
2 garlic cloves, finely chopped
1 1/2 pounds halibut fillet, skin removed
2 tablespoons extra virgin olive oil

1. Heat the oil in a 10-inch skillet over medium heat until hot. Add the anchovies and sauté 30 seconds. Add the wine and simmer 1 minute. Mash the anchovies with the back of a spoon.
2. Pass the contents of the pan through a fine sieve into a bowl, pressing down hard with the back of a spoon.
3. Add the tomatoes to the mixture and bruise them with a potato masher or fork. Stir in the remaining ingredients.
4. Season the halibut with freshly ground black pepper.
5. Wash and dry the skillet. Heat 2 tablespoons olive oil over high heat until hot. Add the fish and sauté 1 minute. Turn the fish over and sauté 30 seconds.
6. Add the tomato mixture, bring to a boil, reduce the heat to medium, and simmer gently 2 minutes. Drizzle with 2 tablespoons olive oil.
7. Cover the pan and remove from the heat. Allow the fish to rest in the pan for 5 to 7 minutes, until cooked through.
8. Place the fillets on warm plates. Spoon the sauce over the fish and serve with spinach mashed potatoes alongside.

Spinach Mashed Potatoes

1 pound yellow-flesh potatoes, peeled and cut into chunks
2 cups packed baby spinach, coarsely chopped
4 tablespoons olive oil
4 teaspoons finely grated Parmesan cheese
2 tablespoons yogurt
2 to 3 scrapes of nutmeg
Kosher salt and freshly ground black pepper

Simmer the potatoes in lightly salted water until tender, 15 to 20 minutes. Drain the potatoes and return them to the pan. Add the spinach and olive oil, Parmesan, yogurt, and nutmeg and mash well. Season with salt and pepper.

Sautéed Lingcod
with Vegetable Tartar

When is a cod not a cod? When it is a lingcod, a deliciously sweet, if decidedly unattractive-looking, fish that makes its home along the western shores of North America, from Vancouver in the north to the Baja peninsula in the south. Kaleidoscopic in color and utterly devoid of carbohydrates, this stunning dish is a favorite.

One 24-ounce lingcod fillet

For the vegetable tartar:
28 haricots verts (slender French green beans)
2 tablespoons finely diced red onion
1 cup finely diced carrot
1/2 cup finely diced outer green of zucchini
1 medium cucumber, peeled, seeded, and finely diced
1 red bell pepper, roasted, peeled , and finely diced
1/2 cup semiripe mango, finely diced
2 teaspoons extra virgin olive oil
1/2 teaspoon lemon juice
The finely grated zest of 1 lemon
1 teaspoon kosher salt and freshly ground black pepper

For the dill vinaigrette:
2 tablespoons yellow mustard
1 tablespoon dill leaves
2 teaspoons red wine vinegar
1/2 cup olive oil

1. Blanch the haricots in lightly salted boiling water for 2 to 3 minutes until bright green and crisp-tender. Chill under cold running water and drain well. Slice the beans on the bias into thin 1/4-inch-long slivers. Reserve for garnish.
2. Mix the remaining diced vegetables and mango in a bowl with olive oil, lemon juice, and zest. Season with salt and pepper.
3. Make the vinaigrette: In a separate bowl combine the mustard vinegar, dill, and olive oil; whisk until creamy.
4. Preheat a nonstick skillet over high heat until hot. Rub both sides of the fish lightly with olive oil. Place the fish in the pan and sear 2 min. Flip the fish and sear 1 minute more, until barely cooked through.
5. To serve: Make a bed of vegetable tartar among 4 plates. Scatter the green beans over the tartar and top with the fish. Spoon the vinaigrette over and around the fish and serve immediately.

Hearty Fish Soup Stew
with Garlic and Parsley Crostini

This light and zesty twist on bouillabaisse, the traditional Marseillaise fish stew, is layered with flavor and color, and redolent of anise, garlic, olives, and tomatoes. Enjoy it at the height of the summer, when the vegetables are at their freshest and it's easy to imagine yourself running your toes through the sands of Provence!

1 pound fingerling potatoes, peeled and sliced in half
1 cup sliced red onion
1 yellow bell pepper, peeled and julienned
1 medium fennel bulb, trimmed and sliced lengthwise 1/4 inch thick
4 large scallions, white and pale green, sliced lengthwise in half
2 medium carrots, peeled and julienned
10 basil leaves
2 celery stalks, strings removed and julienned
12 green olives
6 cornichons, halved lengthwise
4 canned plum tomatoes, drained and chopped (about 1/2 cup)
4 garlic cloves, peeled and quartered
1/2 cup extra virgin olive oil
1 teaspoon salt
1 cup plus 2 tablespoons dry white wine
1 cup juice from tomatoes
1 1/2 pounds assorted firm-fleshed fish fillets, such as halibut, salmon, or lingcod, cut into 2-inch chunks

1. Preheat the oven to 500 degrees F. Simmer the potatoes in lightly salted water for 6 minutes. They should still be quite firm. Drain and set aside.
2. Layer the vegetables in a large sauté pan and turn the heat to high. Add garlic and oil. When the vegetables begin to simmer, lower the heat to medium and sauté, stirring frequently until soft and lightly caramelized, 10 to 12 minutes. Season the vegetables with salt.
3. Lay the potatoes, fish, cornichons, and olives over the vegetables and raise the heat. Simmer for 1 minute. Add 1 cup white wine and 1 cup tomato juice. Transfer pan to the oven for 12 minutes or until the fish is cooked through.
4. Remove pan from the oven and transfer to a serving large bowl. Drizzle the remaining white wine over the stew and surround with crostini (see below). Sprinkle the Parmesan-parsley mixture over the stew and serve.

For the crostini:
12 slices baguette, 1/2 inch thick and 3 inches in length
2 garlic cloves, peeled and cut in half
1 red pepper, peeled, roasted, and finely chopped
1 tablespoon finely chopped parsley
2 tablespoons extra virgin olive oil
1 tablespoon finely grated Parmesan cheese

1. Rub one side of the bread slices with the garlic. Place bread garlic side up on a sheet pan and bake in the oven for 3 to 4 minutes, until lightly toasted.
2. Combine the parsley and Parmesan in a small bowl. In a second bowl, combine the pepper and olive oil. Spread the toast with the peppers and sprinkle with 1/2 of the Parmesan-parsley mixture. Reserve the remaining mixture to garnish the soup. Return the toast to the oven and bake for 2 minutes.

FISH AND CHIPS
WITH AIOLI MOUSSE

Call it comfort food or call it the height of elegance: this very modern and healthy take on everyone's favorite British entrée puts a low-fat spin on a dish that can be traditionally quite heavy. Sophisticated yet hearty, it can be enjoyed on any occasion, from a casual get-together to a chic supper.

For the aioli mousse:
1 quart low-fat milk
Kosher salt
1 head garlic, cloves peeled and halved
1 bay leaf
1/2 cup extra virgin olive oil
1/2 cup heavy cream
1 teaspoon finely chopped lemon zest

For the fish and chips:
4 medium potatoes with skin (about 1 pound)
1 1/2 pounds fish fillet such as pollack, cod, or telapia, cut into 2-inch pieces
Kosher salt and freshly ground black pepper
1/2 cup lemon juice
3 eggs
3 tablespoons white wine
Freshly ground black pepper
3 cups dried bread crumbs
1 large bunch mint, separated into sprigs
1 lemon, cut into 4 wedges

1. Make the aioli mousse: Combine 2 cups milk and a pinch of salt in a small saucepan. Add the garlic and bay leaf to the milk and bring to a boil. Drain the pan and return the garlic and bay leaf to the pan with another 1/2 cup milk. Again bring to a boil and drain, repeating as before, pouring in the milk and reducing to 1/2 cup until you have 1/2 cup milk remaining. Reserve the garlic and discard the bay leaf.

2. Transfer the garlic to a blender. Add 1/4 cup oil and 2 tablespoons of the reserved milk. Puree 1 minute. Add the remaining oil and milk and puree until completely smooth, scraping down the side of the blender several times to incorporate all the garlic. Refrigerate.

3. Pour the cream into a chilled bowl and whip until stiff. Add the garlic puree to the cream and gently whisk to combine. Fold in the lemon zest, season with salt and pepper. Refrigerate the aioli mousse until ready to serve.

4. Make the fish and chips: Slice the potatoes into paper-thin rounds on a mandoline. Submerge the slices in a bowl of cold water and soak for 10 minutes. Stir the slices occasionally to prevent them from sticking together. Transfer the slices to a colander and rinse under cold running water. Drain well and pat dry with paper towels.

5. Marinate the fish in lemon juice for 10 minutes, drain. Season with salt and pepper.

6. In a bowl whisk the eggs with wine until foamy. Season with pepper. Add the fish to the egg mixture and soak 8 to 10 minutes.

7. Heat 6 cups vegetable oil or to the depth of 1 inch in a wide heavy skillet to 360 degrees F.

8. Spread the bread crumbs on a plate. Lift up a piece of fish and allow the egg-wine mixture to drip off, coat with bread crumbs, and transfer to a paper towel. Repeat with remaining fish.

9. Add fish to the oil without overcrowding and fry 2 minutes, turning halfway through. Regulate the heat to maintain the oil at 350 degrees F. Drain the fish to a platter lined with paper towels and fry the remaining fish in the same manner.

10. Add half the potatoes to the oil and fry 1 minute, turning once, until golden brown. Transfer the chips to another paper-towel-lined platter and season lightly with salt. Fry the remaining potatoes in the same manner.

11. Place a dollop of aioli mousse on each of 4 plates. Pile the fish next to the sauce. Garnish each plate with a wedge of lemon and a sprig of mint. Serve immediately.

Serving suggestion: Place 3 to 4 mints sprigs in each of 4 large wineglasses. Arrange a cloth napkin over the mint, then gently put the chips in the glasses.

Baked Turbot Fillet with Fava Beans and Artichoke Puree

Serves 4

Prepared with only a modicum of butter substitute and olive oil, this mouthwatering dish allows the robust flavors of artichoke, marjoram, and fresh fava beans to function as the flavor base for tender, flaky turbot fillet. Silky in texture, it is as much a feast for the eyes as it is for the palate.

2 small potatoes, quartered
1/2 cup chopped onion
2 large artichokes, trimmed to the heart, each heart cut into 4 wedges
4 branches fresh marjoram
2 tablespoons butter
2 tablespoons extra virgin olive oil
Kosher salt and freshly ground black pepper
2 pounds fresh fava beans in the pod (about 2 cups), shelled
1 tablespoon lemon juice
Four 6-ounce skinless turbot fillets

1. Make the artichoke puree: Combine the potatoes, onion, artichokes, marjoram, butter, 1 teaspoon olive oil, 1/4 teaspoon salt, and 1 cup water in a small saucepan. Bring to boil over high heat, then reduce the heat and simmer 18 to 20 minutes, until the artichokes are tender and the potatoes crush easily against the side of the pan when pressed with back of a spoon.
2. Transfer vegetables with cooking water to a blender and puree until smooth. With a rubber spatula pass the puree through a fine-mesh sieve into a bowl. Scrape remaining artichoke from the blender into the bowl, and stir well, adding up to 4 tablespoons water to achieve your desired consistency.
3. Make the fava bean salad: Blanch the beans in lightly salted boiling water for 30 seconds. Transfer the beans to a bowl of ice water until cold. Peel the beans and toss with lemon juice, and 1 tablespoon olive oil. Season with salt and pepper.
4. Rinse the fillets and pat dry. Season both sides with salt and pepper. Heat 2 teaspoons olive oil in a wide nonstick skillet over high heat until hot. Sauté the fillets for 3 minutes on each side, until barely cooked through.
5. To serve: Divide the artichoke puree between 4 warm soup plates. Lay the fish over the puree. Scatter the fava beans over and around the fish.

Tuna Tartar with Broccolini Salad and Pickled Red Onion

Serves 4

The next best thing to preparing sushi at home is creating a tuna tartar that marries the flavors of East and West. Healthy, robustly flavored, and utterly delicious, this dish necessitates that you use the absolute freshest, sushi-grade ahi tuna. The result will be well worth it.

For the tartar:
8 ounces sushi-grade ahi tuna, finely diced
2 teaspoons chopped dill
1/2 teaspoon prepared yellow mustard
4 tablespoons extra virgin olive oil

For the salad:
4 teaspoons extra virgin olive oil
1/2 cup thinly sliced red onion
6 tablespoons red wine vinegar
Kosher salt and freshly ground black pepper
8 stalks broccolini, cut into florets and stems discarded
2 teaspoons lemon juice

1. Chill a bowl in the freezer until cold. Add the diced tuna, dill, mustard, and 4 tablespoons olive oil and combine well. Return it to the refrigerator until ready to serve.
2. Combine 2 teaspoons olive oil and the onions in a small skillet and sauté over medium heat for 2 minutes. Add the vinegar and simmer 3 to 4 minutes, until most of the liquid has reduced but the onions remain juicy. Season with salt and pepper and set aside.
3. Blanch the broccolini florets in lightly salted boiling water for 3 minutes. Transfer to a bowl of ice water until cold. Drain well and pat dry.
4. Toss the florets in a bowl with 2 teaspoons oil and lemon juice, and season again with salt and pepper.
5. Mound the tartar on each of 4 chilled salad plates. Scatter the broccolini around the tartar and garnish with onions and dill.

Sautéed Black Sea Bass
with Black Olive and Eggplant Puree

Serves 4

A richly aromatic and healthful meal fit for the likes of King David, this luxurious dish is ripe with the flavors of the Middle East, and another kosher billionaire favorite. If you can't find black sea bass at your local fish market, substitute halibut or any firm-fleshed white fish.

2 medium eggplants, about 3/4 pound each, peeled and cut into 2-inch
    chunks
4 garlic cloves, peeled and lightly bruised with the side of a knife
Kosher salt and freshly ground black pepper
2 tablespoons plus 2 teaspoons extra virgin olive oil
2 tablespoons lemon juice
1/2 cup store-bought Israeli-style hummus
Four 6-ounce black sea bass fillets, skin removed
2 garlic cloves, finely chopped
2 tablespoons chopped parsley
2/3 cup pitted kalamata olives
1 cup dry white wine
2 tablespoons unsalted butter
6 small sprigs fresh herbs such as thyme, tarragon, rosemary, and oregano

1. Preheat the oven to 400 degrees F. Spread the eggplant and 4 garlic cloves on a baking sheet. Toss with 2 teaspoons olive oil and season lightly with salt and pepper. Place a rack in the middle of the oven and bake for 20 to 25 minutes, until the eggplant is lightly browned and begins to collapse. Discard the garlic and transfer the eggplant to a food processor. Add the lemon juice and 1 tablespoon olive oil and pulse to a coarse puree. With a rubber spatula, pass the puree through a fine sieve into a bowl. Stir in the hummus and set aside.
2. Season the fillets with salt and pepper. Heat 1 tablespoon olive oil in a wide nonstick sauté pan over medium-high heat until hot. Add the fish and sauté 3 minutes per side or until cooked through. Transfer the fish to a warmed serving plate.
3. Wipe out the pan, add 1 tablespoon olive oil to the pan, and return it to high heat. Add the finely chopped garlic, parsley, olives, and wine. Stir in butter, 1 tablespoon of the eggplant puree, and the herb sprigs. Simmer for 2 minutes and remove from the heat.
4. To serve: Make a circle of eggplant puree in the center of each of 4 warm plates. Arrange a fillet of fish over the puree. Place 5 olives on and around the fish. Spoon the pan sauce over the fish.

MEAT AND POULTRY

BEEF BORDEAUX
WITH CREAMY SAFFRON POTATO PUREE

Serves 4

Aromatic and deeply fragrant with essences of red wine and herbs, this velvety-rich authentic French stew is as welcome at an opulent cool-weather dinner party as it is at a romantic supper for two in front of a roaring fire.

2 tablespoons extra virgin olive oil
2 medium carrots, sliced into 1-inch pieces
6 celery stalks, sliced into 1-inch pieces
2 large onions, peeled and roughly chopped
2 garlic cloves, peeled and halved
2 marjoram sprigs
2 thyme sprigs
3 bay leaves
1 1/2 pounds beef chuck, cut into 3-inch pieces
Kosher salt and freshly ground black pepper
4 teaspoons all-purpose flour
2 tablespoons vegetable oil
4 cups red wine
4 plum tomatoes, quartered
1 teaspoon dried green peppercorns
1 teaspoon turmeric
2 tablespoons chopped parsley

1. Heat the olive oil in a 2- to 3-quart saucepan over high heat. Add the carrots, celery, onions, garlic, herbs, and bay leaves and sauté for 3 to 4 minutes, until the vegetables are lightly browned. Remove from heat.
2. Season the meat with salt and pepper, then dust with flour.
3. Heat the vegetable oil in a heavy, wide skillet over medium-high heat until hot. Add the beef and brown on all sides, about 2 to 3 minutes, regulating the heat to prevent scorching. Add 1 cup wine to the pan and scrape up any caramelized bits from the bottom with a wooden spoon or rubber spatula. Transfer the meat and pan juice to the vegetables.
4. Add the tomatoes, peppercorns, turmeric, and remaining 3 cups wine. Turn the heat to high and bring to a boil.
5. Lower the heat and cook at a gentle simmer, uncovered, for 2 hours, until the meat is fork-tender. Add more wine if the meat threatens to dry out before it is done cooking.

Saffron Potato Puree

No one will ever believe how healthy this rich and creamy puree is! A natural accompaniment to the Beef Bordeaux, it also goes perfectly with a simple roasted or broiled fish.

1/4 teaspoon saffron threads
2 tablespoons hot water
2 tablespoons plus 2 teaspoons extra virgin olive oil
4 teaspoons salt
4 medium potatoes (about 2 pounds), peeled and quartered
4 teaspoons butter substitute
Freshly ground black pepper
4 tablespoons unflavored organic soy milk

1. Combine the saffron, hot water, and olive oil in a small dish.
2. Simmer the potatoes in lightly salted water to cover for 15 to 20 minutes or until they pierce easily with the tip of a knife.
3. Drain the potatoes and return them to the pan. Over low heat, add the saffron and butter and mash with a fork.
4. Add the soy milk and whisk until smooth. Season with salt and pepper.

To serve: Spoon the potato puree onto warm plates. Arrange chunks of beef over the puree. Spoon the stew vegetables over and around the beef. Drizzle each plate with the braising liquid and garnish with chopped parsley.

Beef Chop
with Herbed Artichoke Potatoes
Serves 4

This modern take on the traditional Tuscan chop pan-roasted with herbs, potatoes, and artichokes is home-style cooking elevated to luxurious. The strong flavors of the herbs and artichokes are set off by the succulent steak, for a delectable result.

8 baby artichokes, trimmed of tough outer leaves
1/2 pound unpeeled fingerling potatoes, sliced 1/2 inch thick
2 tablespoons butter substitute or olive oil
4 porterhouse chops, 1 inch thick, bones scraped clean
Kosher salt and freshly ground black pepper
4 tablespoons chopped flat-leaf parsley leaves
2 large garlic cloves, unpeeled and lightly crushed
Two 3-inch rosemary sprigs
2/3 cup dry white wine
2/3 cup water
1/2 cup chicken broth reduced to 4 table spoons

1. Slice each artichoke into 4 wedges. Simmer in water to cover for 5 minutes until tender, drain well.
2. In a separate pan cover the potatoes with water and simmer 10 minutes until tender, drain well.
3. Heat the butter substitute or oil in an 8- to 10-inch-wide skillet over medium heat until hot. Season the chops all over with salt and pepper. Place the chops in the pan and sear on one side for 2 minutes until golden brown. Turn the chops. Add the parsley leaves, garlic clove, rosemary, potatoes, and artichokes. Add white wine, water, and chicken broth. Raise the heat and bring to a simmer, regulate the heat to maintain a steady simmer for 7 to 8 minutes until the beef is cooked through and the sauce has reduced. Discard the rosemary.
4. To serve: Divide the potatoes and artichokes on each of 4 warm plates. Arrange the chops over the vegetables. Spoon the sauce over and around the chops. Serve immediately.

Pan-Roasted Chicken
with Wild Rice and Chanterelles
Serves 4

This dish draws on the famous poulet d'Auvergne for inspiration; what it lacks in fat it makes up for with the astounding earthy flavors of herbs, chanterelles, and wild rice. A monumental classic.

1 cup wild rice
3 cups water
1/2 teaspoon kosher salt
2 large whole skinless boneless chicken breasts (12 to 14 ounces each), split in half
4 tablespoons mixed chopped herbs such as rosemary, sage, thyme, and basil
4 teaspoons olive oil
2 garlic cloves, crushed and finely chopped
12 flat-leaf parsley leaves, coarsely chopped
12 ounces chanterelle mushrooms, rinsed in warm water, large stems peeled, and halved if large, left whole if small
1/2 cup dry white wine
1/2 cup chicken stock
10 ounces baby spinach
1 teaspoon butter substitute

1. Preheat the oven to 400 degrees F. Combine rice, water, and salt in a small saucepan and bring to a boil over high heat. Reduce the heat and simmer, covered, for 45 minutes or until the water has been absorbed and the rice is tender. Turn off the heat when done and keep the rice warm.
2. Butterfly each breast half and place skin side down on a clean surface. Season each half with salt and pepper and 1 tablespoon of herbs.
3. Roll up each breast and tie with kitchen twine or secure with toothpicks.
4. Heat 2 teaspoons olive oil in an 8-inch nonstick skillet over high heat until hot. Sear the chicken, rotating frequently for 1 to 2 minutes, until golden brown all over. Remove from the heat.
5. In another ovenproof skillet warm the remaining olive oil over medium heat. Add the garlic and parsley and sauté for 30 seconds. Add the mushrooms and sauté 3 minutes, until tender.
6. Place the chicken on top of the mushrooms. Add the white wine and stock and bring to a boil. Place the pan in the oven and roast 15 to 20 minutes until the chicken is cooked through.
7. When ready to serve, heat the butter substitute in a 12-inch skillet over medium heat until hot. Add the spinach and cook, stirring, for 1 to 2 minutes until wilted, and season with salt and pepper.
8. To serve: Spoon the wild rice into 4 warm soup plates. Top with spinach. Slice each chicken breast on an angle into 1/2-inch-thick rounds. Arrange the chicken over the spinach, spoon the pan sauce and mushrooms over all.

HAMBURGERS
WITH OVEN-FRIED POTATOES AND COLESLAW

Serves 4

Sometimes even the most decadent billionaire needs a little comfort food! At six ounces per patty, each burger is less than the size of a quarter-pounder, and packed with fresh garden riches, from butter lettuce to ripe tomato. With healthy oven fries, it's a perfect main course for a relaxed evening on the patio.

1 1/2 pounds ground beef
4 teaspoons finely chopped shallot
2 teaspoons ketchup
2 teaspoons prepared yellow mustard
4 whole wheat burger buns
4 slices ripe tomato
4 leaves butter lettuce
4 thin slices red onion
Ketchup and Dijon mustard for serving

1. Place the beef, shallot, ketchup, and mustard in a bowl and mix gently until just combined. Form the mixture into 2 patties. Grill or sauté the burgers over medium heat, 4 minutes per side for medium rare.
2. Lightly toast the buns and assemble the burgers with lettuce, tomato, red onion, and ketchup and mustard if desired. Serve with fries and coleslaw (see below).

Oven-Fried Potatoes

1 1/2 pounds Yukon gold potatoes, peeled and cut into 1/2-inch-thick sticks
3 tablespoons olive oil or butter substitute
Salt and freshly ground black pepper

1. Simmer the potatoes in lightly salted water to cover for 6 minutes, until nearly cooked through but still firm. Drain.
2. Spread the potatoes in a roasting pan and dot with butter. Bake for 12 to 14 minutes, turning halfway through, until golden brown and crispy. Season with salt and pepper.

Coleslaw

No more limp coleslaw! In this gloriously healthy dish we've omitted the traditional mayonnaise and replaced it with a light champagne vinaigrette. The result is tangy, crunchy, and perfectly refreshing.

1/4 teaspoon sugar
1/4 teaspoon kosher salt
2 teaspoons champagne vinegar
2 teaspoons chopped dill
2 teaspoons finely chopped chives
1 teaspoon extra virgin olive oil
3 cups thinly sliced cabbage

In a bowl, combine the sugar, salt, vinegar, dill, and chives. Stir in the oil, add the cabbage, and toss well. Refrigerate until cold.

SPICY CHICKEN PAPRIKASH
WITH VEGETABLE TAGLIATELLE

Evocative of the spicy flavors and colors of Morocco, this magnificent dish is everything a billionaire could ask for: healthy, beautiful, and guaranteed to wow dinner guests. Served with an all-vegetable, no-carb take on tagliatelli, it is low in fat and calories and virtually carbohydrate-free. If you have any leftovers (and it's so delicious you likely won't), rejoice: this dish actually gains flavor after spending an overnight in the refrigerator.

4 tablespoons vegetable oil
3 cups thinly sliced onion
2 bay leaves
4 garlic cloves, peeled and left whole
2 teaspoons kosher salt
4 teaspoons flour
4 whole chicken legs, split into drumsticks and thighs
Eight 1/4-inch-thick round lemon slices
1 teaspoon Moroccan tagine spice blend or curry powder
4 tablespoons sweet paprika
3 cups dry red wine
3 cups chicken stock
2/3 cup tomato juice
Two 3-inch rosemary sprigs wrapped in cheesecloth or tied with kitchen twine

1. Heat 2 tablespoons vegetable oil in a heavy 4- to 5-quart casserole over medium heat until hot. Add the onion, bay leaves, and garlic and sauté for 10 minutes or until lightly caramelized.
2. Sprinkle half the salt and half the flour over a paper towel and lay the chicken skin side down. Sprinkle the chicken with the remaining salt and flour.
3. Heat 1 tablespoon oil in a 10-inch skillet over medium-high heat until hot. Add half of the chicken pieces skin side down and cook 3 minutes or until golden brown. Turn the chicken and cook 2 to 3 minutes more. Wipe out the skillet, heat 1 tablespoon oil, and sauté the remaining chicken in the same manner.
4. Transfer the chicken to the casserole. Lay lemon slices over the chicken and sprinkle with spice blend and paprika.
5. Raise the heat to medium and simmer 1 minute until fragrant. Add the wine, stock, tomato juice, and rosemary.
6. Reduce the heat to a gentle simmer and cook, covered, for 35 to 40 minutes, turning the chicken pieces halfway through.

Vegetable Tagliatelle

Your pasta-loving guests won't miss their beloved carbohydrates when you serve our colorful vegetable tagliatelle. Made with the freshest vegetables perfectly julienned, the result is sweet, tender, and al dente.

2 cups cleaned, julienned snow peas
2 cups peeled, julienned daikon radish
2 cups peeled, julienned carrot
4 large zucchini, outer green julienned
4 tablespoons butter substitute
Kosher salt and freshly ground black pepper

1. Prepare a large bowl of ice water.
2. Bring a large pan of lightly salted water to a boil. Add the vegetables and blanch for 2 1/2 minutes or until tender. Drain the vegetables and transfer them to the ice bath to stop their cooking. Drain well and set aside.
3. Heat the butter in a 10- to 12-inch skillet over high heat until foamy. Add the vegetables and season with salt and pepper. Sauté for 2 minutes, stirring frequently, until crisp-tender.

To serve: Transfer the vegetables to 4 warm plates. Place the chicken paprikash on top of the vegetables, heaping the onions over the chicken. Spoon the sauce around the vegetables.

Beef Carpaccio with Fresh Figs and Shaved Vegetable Salad

Serves 4 as an appetizer, 2 as a main course

Light yet satisfying, and laden with the ancient, fresh flavors of Italy, this dish benefits from the finest-quality beef you can find, along with the ripest figs and the oldest balsamic vinegar. Serve it to your guests and you'll all be whisked away to the sandy beaches of the Italian Riviera.

2/3 cup aged balsamic vinegar, preferably 12 years old
1/2 teaspoon honey
5 ripe black mission figs, peeled
8 ounces beef fillet, trimmed of all excess surface fat and thinly sliced
Kosher salt and freshly ground black pepper
5 teaspoons extra virgin olive oil
Juice of 1/2 lemon
1 pimiento or piquillo pepper, sliced into thin strips
1 fennel bulb, trimmed and shaved paper thin
1 medium head frisée, washed and torn into bite-size pieces
1/2 bunch watercress, tough stems discarded
3 cups loosely packed mesclun greens

1. Combine the vinegar and honey in a small saucepan. Boil over high heat until reduced to 1/4 cup. Transfer to a bowl to cool.
2. Place 3 peeled figs in a bowl and mash to a puree with a fork. Slice the remaining figs into quarters and reserve for garnish.
3. Spread 1 teaspoon fig puree on each of 4 chilled plates. Arrange the beef slices in a single layer over the puree. Season the meat with salt and pepper and several drops of olive oil and drizzle with lemon juice.
4. Lay the pimiento strips over the beef and spread with remaining fig puree.
5. Combine the fennel and salad greens in a bowl. Season lightly with salt and pepper and toss with 4 teaspoons olive oil.
6. Mound the salad over the beef. Garnish each plate with 2 sections of fig and drizzle with 1 teaspoon reduced balsamic vinegar. Serve at once.

Polpette with Couscous

Serves 4

Traditionally larger than the average American meatball, polpette are the real thing, often served on their own as a separate course in Italy. Here, carbs are kept to a minimum by swapping the expected pasta with the more refined couscous, for a surprisingly lusty result.

1 pound ground beef
4 tablespoons finely chopped parsley
1/4 teaspoon kosher salt
2 teaspoons dried bread crumbs
6 to 8 scrapings of fresh nutmeg
4 tablespoons extra virgin olive oil
1 cup finely chopped onion
2 garlic cloves, finely chopped
Freshly ground black pepper
1/2 cup dry red wine
1 cup Billionaire's Classic Red Sauce (page 185)
1 cup beef stock

1. Combine the beef, parsley, salt, bread crumbs, and nutmeg. Form the meat into 24 balls, about 1 inch each.
2. Heat the olive oil in a wide skillet over medium-high heat until hot. Add the onions and garlic and sauté for 2 minutes, until wilted. Season with pepper. Add the polpette in batches and cook, stirring, for 2 minutes or until lightly browned all over. Add the wine and bring to boil. Add the sauce and beef stock. Simmer over low heat for 8 to 10 minutes, until the meat is cooked through and the sauce has reduced.
3. Divide the couscous among four warm soup plates and top with polpette. Spoon the onions and sauce over the polpette and serve.

For the couscous:
1 cup instant couscous
1 teaspoon olive oil
1/4 teaspoon salt
1 cup plus 1 tablespoon boiling water

Place the couscous, olive oil, and salt in a small bowl. Stir in the boiling water. Cover the bowl and set aside for 10 minutes, until all the liquid has been absorbed and the couscous is tender. Fluff with a fork and serve.

Braised Beef Cheeks
with Salsa Verde, Horseradish, and Mixed Baby Greens

Serves 4

Long considered a delicacy among the royalty of Europe, beef cheeks are in fact a rustic dish traditionally prized by peasant cooks for their buttery texture and deep flavor. In this magnificent dish, the richness of the beef cheeks is offset by a tangy, robust sauce and tender baby greens for a modern twist on the classic *salade composée*.

1 large fresh sage stem
One 3-inch rosemary sprig
1 pound beef cheeks, trimmed of excess fat
10 cups cold water
3 celery stalks with leaves, halved
2 medium carrots, halved
1 large onion, peeled and cut in half
1 Roma tomato, halved
2 whole cloves
2 juniper berries
1 teaspoon whole black peppercorns
1 bay leaf
1 tablespoon kosher salt

1. Lay the herbs on the meat and roll up. Tie the meat securely with kitchen twine.
2. Combine the water, vegetables, spices and salt in a 4- to 6-quart-saucepan. Bring to a simmer over medium heat.
3. Add the meat and simmer gently for 2 to 2 1/2 hours, skimming frequently when a scum appears on the surface. Add additional water when necessary to keep the meat submerged. The meat is done when it no longer resists the tip of a knife.
4. Transfer the meat to a dish and strain the liquid over it. Chill uncovered in the refrigerator until cold.

For the salad:
2 cups green beans, trimmed
1 cup thinly sliced red onion
1 cup finely chopped celery hearts with leaves
2 tablespoons prepared horseradish
4 tablespoons extra virgin olive oil
4 anchovy fillets packed in oil, drained and finely chopped
2 teaspoons prepared yellow mustard
2 tablespoons lemon juice
Kosher salt and freshly ground black pepper
1 head Boston lettuce, leaves separated, washed, and dried
2 tablespoons chopped parsley

1. Blanch the green beans in lightly salted boiling water until crisp-tender and bright green. Transfer the beans to a bowl of ice water and chill. Drain well and slice into 1-inch lengths.
2. In a bowl, combine the onions, celery, horseradish, olive oil, anchovies, mustard, and lemon juice. Mix well.
3. Untie the meat and discard the herbs. Slice the meat into 1/2-inch chunks and add it to the salad. Add the green beans. Toss well and season with salt and pepper.
4. Chill the salad for 1 hour to allow the flavors to marry.
5. To serve: Line each of 4 plates with several leaves of Bibb lettuce. Spoon the beef salad over the lettuce and sprinkle with chopped parsley.

Roast Stuffed Shoulder of Lamb
with Grilled Zucchini and Celery Root Puree

Serves 4 as an appetizer, 2 as a main course

From the sun-dappled island of Santorini to the palm-shaded cities of Israel and every Mediterranean locale in between, sweet, tender lamb is ubiquitous, with a deep spiritual connection to virtually every religion on earth. This luscious slow-roasted treat is pure culinary ecstasy when paired with grilled zucchini and this healthy take on mashed potatoes, a light celery root puree.

1/3 cup loosely packed finely chopped mixed herbs, such as tarragon, thyme, and rosemary
2 garlic cloves, finely chopped
2 pounds boneless lamb shoulder, trimmed of excess fat
Kosher salt and freshly ground black pepper
1 tablespoon extra virgin olive oil
1 tablespoon butter substitute
2 medium carrots, cut into 1-inch chunks
2 celery stalks, cut into 1-inch chunks
1 large red onion, cut into 1-inch chunks
1 1/4 cups dry white wine

1. Preheat the oven to 400 degrees F. Spread the chopped garlic-herb mixture over the lamb and season with salt and plenty of pepper. Roll the meat and tie with kitchen twine.
2. Heat the extra virgin olive oil and butter substitute in a heavy ovenproof skillet over high heat until hot. Add the vegetables and sauté 1 minute. Add the meat and sear for 3 minutes on each side, turning occasionally, until well browned all over.
3. Add the wine and transfer the pan to the oven. Roast for 20 minutes. Lower the oven to 300 degrees F. Add 1/2 cup water and turn the lamb over. Cover the pan with foil and roast for 2 hours or until the lamb is fork-tender. Prepare the celery root puree and zucchini while the lamb roasts. Remove the lamb from the oven and allow it to rest until serving.

Celery Root Puree

Celery root is an unfairly neglected treat, but it is packed with vitamins and the fresh flavor of sweet celery, a treat accompaniment to potatoes, and virtually ideal as a complementary mash. Serve this with lamb or with any grilled or roasted meat or poultry.

1 tablespoon butter substitute
1 small or 1/2 large celery root, peeled (about 8 ounces)
1 small peeled potato (about 4 ounces)
Kosher salt and freshly ground black pepper

Heat the butter substitute in a small saucepan over medium heat until hot. Add the celery root and potato. Season with a pinch of salt and a few grinds of pepper and sauté 2 minutes. Add 1 cup water. Bring to a simmer and cook for 20 minutes, until the vegetables crush easily against the side of the pan when pressed with the back of a spoon. Transfer the contents of the pan to a blender and puree until smooth.

Grilled Zucchini

1 pound zucchini, sliced on the bias into 1/2-inch-thick pieces
2 teaspoons extra virgin olive oil
Kosher salt and freshly ground black pepper

Toss the zucchini in olive oil and season with salt and pepper. Heat a grill pan over medium heat until hot. Lay the zucchini in the pan and grill for 2 minutes on each side or until lightly browned.

To serve: Untie the lamb and slice into 4 portions. Spoon the celery root puree onto warm plates. Place the lamb on top of the puree. Spoon the braising liquid over the lamb. Arrange the zucchini on the side.

BEEF RAGÙ WITH EGGPLANT TIMBALE AND FRESH PEA PUREE

Serves 4

This visually stunning, mouthwatering, modern ragù melds the traditional flavors of Italy with the bright green, earth-ripe flavor of sweet, pureed peas. Seek out the youngest peas you can find: the texture and taste are incomparable.

4 small eggplants, about 8 ounces each
1 cup all-purpose flour
Vegetable oil
1 pound boneless loin of beef, cut into 1/2-inch cubes
2 tablespoons extra virgin olive oil
Kosher salt and freshly ground black pepper
1/2 cup finely chopped onion
1 cup finely chopped celery
1 cup finely chopped carrot
2 teaspoons finely chopped rosemary
2 garlic cloves, finely chopped
1 cup dry white wine
1 cup beef or chicken stock
1 cup peeled, seeded, diced plum tomatoes

1. Preheat the oven to 400 degrees F. Trim the ends from the eggplant. Peel away 1/2-inch-wide strips of skin. Cut lengthwise into 16 slices, 1/4 inch thick.
2. Reserve 4 teaspoons of the flour for the ragù and spread the rest on a plate. Press each side of the eggplant slices lightly in the flour. Shake off excess.
3. Place a medium skillet over medium-high heat. Add vegetable oil to the depth of 1/2 inch. When the oil is hot, add the eggplant and fry for 1 to 2 minutes per side, until golden brown and tender. Transfer the eggplant to a paper-towel-lined plate to drain. Season with salt and pepper.
4. Make the ragù: Heat the olive oil in a 3- to 4-quart casserole over medium heat until hot. Add the vegetables, rosemary, and garlic and sauté 2 minutes.
5. Dust the beef chunks with the reserved flour and season with salt and pepper. Add the beef to the vegetables and sauté 2 minutes, until lightly browned.
6. Add the wine and stock and simmer 3 to 4 minutes, until the liquid has reduced and the beef is tender. Remove from the heat and set aside.
7. Assemble the timbale: Line four 8-ounce soufflé molds or ramekins each with 4 slices of eggplant, draping the eggplant over the sides.
8. Make a layer of diced tomatoes on the bottom of each mold and fill up with ragù. Fold the sides of the eggplant over the top.
9. Transfer the molds to a shallow roasting pan. Place the roasting pan on a rack in the middle of the oven and pour boiling water around the molds to come halfway up their sides. Bake for 10 minutes.

10. Run a thin knife blade or spatula around the inside of each mold to loosen the eggplant. Invert the timbales onto 4 warm plates. Spoon the pea puree (see below) around the timbales and serve immediately.

Fresh Pea Puree

The key to cooking with peas and maintaining their emerald-green color and earthy flavor is to buy them when they are fresh and shell them in your own kitchen (a great job for tiny hands: give the little ones a bowl, and let them enjoy themselves!). Fresh pea puree is a surprising treat that provides a bright flavor and textural counterpoint to whatever it's served with: it even does double duty as a healthy dip for toasted pita!

3 cups shelled sweet peas
1/2 cup thinly sliced onion
2 teaspoons butter substitute
1 1/2 cups water
1/2 teaspoon kosher salt and freshly ground black pepper
4 scrapes of nutmeg
2 tiny pinches ground cinnamon

Combine all the ingredients in a small saucepan. Simmer over medium heat, until the peas crush easily against the side of the pan when pressed with a spoon. Transfer the contents of the pan to a blender and puree until smooth.

Seared Duck Breast
with Shiitake Mushrooms
and Honey Lime Ginger Sauce

Serves 4 as an appetizer, 2 as a main course

A treat that sometimes goes overlooked, duck is redolent of sweet gaminess without being overpowering; lower in fat and cholesterol than red meat, it is a perfect foil for the delicious Asian fusion of mushrooms, lime, and ginger.

4 duck breasts with skin, about 8 ounces each
Kosher salt and freshly ground black pepper
2 teaspoons butter substitute
1 teaspoon vegetable oil
1 tablespoon fresh ginger, peeled and finely chopped
4 tablespoons Armagnac or brandy
2 tablespoons lime juice
4 tablespoons honey
2 tablespoons organic soy sauce
2 teaspoons extra virgin olive oil
8 ounce shiitake mushrooms, stems discarded
32 snow peas, strings removed, and julienned
2/3 cup chicken stock
2 ripe plums, sliced into wedges
2 scallions, thinly sliced

1. Score the duck skin in a crosshatch pattern with a sharp knife. Season with salt and pepper.
2. Heat 1 teaspoon butter substitute and oil in a skillet over medium heat until hot. Add the duck breasts skin side down and sear for 2 minutes. Turn the breasts and sear 2 minutes more. Transfer the duck to a plate and discard the fat in the skillet. Wash and dry the skillet and return to medium heat.
3. Heat the remaining tablespoon butter substitute and ginger together and sauté 30 seconds. Add the Armagnac, lime juice, honey, and soy sauce. Raise the heat and simmer 1 minute. Transfer the sauce to a small bowl.
4. Wash and dry the pan and return it to medium heat. Add the olive oil, mushrooms, and snow peas. Raise the heat to high and stir-fry the vegetables for 1 minute.
5. Place the duck skin side down over the vegetables and simmer 1 minute. Add the reserved sauce and stock. Turn the breast skin side up. Simmer 2 minutes, until the sauce reduces.
6. Transfer the duck to a roasting pan and roast in the oven for 4 minutes, until medium rare. Transfer the duck to a cutting board and let rest for 2 minutes.
7. With a slotted spoon transfer the vegetables to 4 warm plates. Slice the duck and fan it out over the vegetables. Spoon the sauce over and around the duck. Garnish with plum wedges and scallions.

MEAT SUBSTITUTES

Seitan Braised in Red Wine with Sage and Onions

Serves 4

Rich, dense, and toothsome, this vegan twist on a very traditional braise will thrill even the most die-hard meat eaters.

2 medium onions, peeled and diced in 1/2-inch chunks
1 medium carrot, sliced 1/2 inch thick
1 celery stalk, sliced 1/2 inch thick
1 pound seitan, cut into 1-inch chunks
6 large sage leaves
1 cup dry red wine
1/3 cup balsamic vinegar
3 tablespoons extra virgin olive oil
1/4 cup soy sauce
1 tablespoon honey
1 tablespoon finely chopped parsley

1. Preheat the oven to 475 degrees F.
2. In a large ovenproof sauté pan or 3-quart casserole arrange the onions, carrots, and celery in a single layer. Add the seitan and sage.
3. In a small bowl, whisk together the wine, vinegar, olive oil, soy sauce, and honey with 1/3 cup of water. Pour the mixture evenly over the onions and seitan. Place the pan over high heat and bring to a boil.
4. Transfer the pan to the oven and roast for 25 minutes, stirring occasionally for even browning.
5. Garnish with chopped parsley and serve over steamed brown rice, mashed potatoes, or wilted spinach.

Baked Millet with Sweet Potato Croquettes and Tangy Yogurt Sauce

Serves 4

Everyone's favorite potato croquettes are elevated to exquisite status in this dish that enriches the tender sweet potato with protein-rich millet and lentils. Yogurt sauce provides the high counterpoint to a dish that can replace virtually any meat- or poultry-based entrée.

1/2 cup millet
1/4 cup red lentils
1/2 cup sushi rice
1 tablespoon white sesame seeds
1 cup finely chopped sweet potato
2 celery stalks, finely diced
4 scallions, thinly sliced
1 garlic clove, minced
1-inch piece fresh ginger, peeled and minced
2 tablespoons extra virgin olive oil plus additional for brushing croquettes
Kosher salt and freshly ground black pepper
1/4 cup finely chopped fresh parsley

1. Preheat the oven to 400 degrees F. In a 2-quart saucepan over high heat, combine the millet, lentils, rice, and sesame seeds with 3 cups of water and 1/2 teaspoon of salt. Bring to a boil. Reduce the heat to low, cover, and simmer for 35 minutes, until all the water has been absorbed.
2. While the grains cook, sauté the vegetables, garlic, and ginger in 2 tablespoons of olive oil over medium heat for 3 to 4 minutes until softened. Add 1/2 teaspoon salt and 2 tablespoons water. Cover the pan, reduce the heat to low, and simmer until the vegetables are tender, about 5 to 7 minutes. Transfer the vegetables to a mixing bowl.
3. Add the grains to the vegetables mix thoroughly and set aside to cool. Stir in the parsley and black pepper.
4. Line a baking sheet with parchment paper. With moist hands, form the croquettes, using 1/2 cup of the mixture for each. Place the an inch apart on the baking sheet and brush lightly with olive oil.
5. Bake for 20 minutes, until they are golden brown and crispy. Serve with yogurt sauce (page 218) on the side.

Moroccan-Style Chickpea and Vegetable Tagine

Serves 4

This dish speaks of warm, balmy nights in Casablanca, where the aromas of ancient spices enchant the senses. Deceptively simple to make, it will leave guests clamoring for more.

For the spice mixture:
2 teaspoons cumin seeds
1 teaspoon caraway seeds
1 teaspoon coriander seeds
1/2 teaspoon whole black peppercorns
1/2 cinnamon stick
1/2 teaspoon paprika
1/2 teaspoon cayenne pepper

For the tagine:
2 tablespoons extra virgin olive oil
2 medium onions, diced
2 medium carrots, diced
2 garlic cloves, peeled and left whole
2 teaspoons kosher salt, plus additional to taste
1 medium sweet potato, peeled and diced
2 cups chopped green cabbage
1 1/2 cups water
One 14-ounce can diced tomatoes (with their juice)
One 14-ounce can chickpeas, drained
Lemon juice if desired
Chopped fresh cilantro, parsley, or chives for garnish

1. Combine the spices in an electric spice mill or coffee mill and grind to a powder.
2. Warm the oil in a 3-quart heavy-bottomed saucepan over medium heat. Add the onions, carrots, celery, garlic, and salt. Raise the heat and bring to a simmer. Cover the pan, reduce heat to low, and cook for 20 minutes.
3. Add the spice mixture to the vegetables along with the cabbage, water, tomatoes, and chickpeas. Raise the heat and bring to a boil. Reduce the heat to low and simmer, uncovered, for 20 to 30 minutes or until the vegetables are tender and the tagine has thickened.
4. Adjust the seasonings with salt or a squeeze of lemon juice to taste. Serve over couscous or rice and sprinkle with cilantro, parsley, or chives.

Tempeh Braised in White Wine with Garlic and Fresh Herbs

Serves 4

Few soy products hold up to braising as well as tempeh, making this dish a perfect, flavor-packed vegan substitute for any herby pan roast.

2 tablespoons olive oil
One 8-ounce package soy tempeh, sliced into bite-size pieces
1/4 cup dry white wine
1 tablespoon soy sauce
1 medium onion, peeled and diced
12 ounces chanterelle mushrooms, left whole or halved if large
2 teaspoons unbleached white all-purpose flour
1 cup vegetable stock (page 190)
8 very fresh garlic cloves, peeled and left whole
Bouquet garni of 2 fresh thyme sprigs, 1 parsley sprig, and a small handful of celery leaves, tied together with kitchen twine or wrapped in a cheesecloth bundle
Kosher salt and freshly ground black pepper
Chopped parsley for garnish

1. Heat 1 tablespoon of the oil in a heavy 8- to 10-inch sauté pan over medium heat until hot. Add the tempeh and sauté until golden brown on all sides, about 8 minutes. Add the wine and soy sauce, raise the heat, and bring to a boil. Cook until the liquid is reduced to half its original volume. Turn the contents of the pan into a bowl and set aside.
2. Add the remaining 1 tablespoon of oil to the pan. Add the onions and mushrooms and sauté over medium-high heat, stirring and tossing for 8 to 10 minutes, until the vegetables are lightly caramelized. Stir in the flour and cook 1 minute, until the flour smells toasted and fragrant.
3. Add the vegetable stock, garlic, and bouquet garni and bring to a boil. With a wooden spoon, scrape up any browned bits that cling to the bottom of the pan. Reduce the heat to low and add the tempeh along with any juices that have collected in the bowl.
4. Cover the pan and simmer gently for 30 minutes. Uncover the pan and continue to cook until the liquid thickens into a sauce. Remove the bouquet garni. Season the tempeh with salt and pepper, sprinkle with chopped parsley, and serve.

PAN-SEARED SEITAN SALAD

Rich, flavorful, and laden with healthy flavors and textures, this warm seitan salad can do duty either as an appetizer, a salad course, or a main course.

1 pound seitan, gently squeezed to remove excess liquid, sliced 1/2 inch
   thick
Freshly squeezed juice of 1 1/2 lemons

For the marinade:
6 tablespoons extra virgin olive oil
3 tablespoons naturally brewed soy sauce
3 tablespoons mirin
1 tablespoon plus 1 1/2 teaspoons Dijon mustard
1 tablespoon finely chopped thyme leaves
3 garlic cloves, crushed to a paste or finely grated
Finely grated zest of 1 1/2 lemons
3/4 teaspoon sea salt or kosher salt
Freshly ground black pepper

1. Combine the marinade ingredients in a medium bowl. Add the seitan and toss until well combined.
2. In a small dish, combine the lemon juice with 2 tablespoons water.
3. Heat a cast-iron or other heavy, 8- to 10-inch skillet over high heat until hot. Pour the seitan and all of the marinade into the pan, reduce the heat to medium, and cook undisturbed until the seitan is nicely browned on the bottom, about 2 minutes. Flip the seitan pieces and cook until browned on the second side, about 2 minutes more. Turn off the heat.
4. Transfer the seitan to a platter. Pour the lemon and water mixture into the pan, scraping up all the caramelized bits from the bottom of the pan with a wooden spoon. Pour this pan sauce over the seitan. Set aside while you make the salad.

For the salad:
2 cups green beans, trimmed
1 cup thinly sliced red onion
1 cup celery hearts with leaves, finely chopped
2 tablespoons prepared horseradish
4 tablespoons extra virgin olive oil
4 anchovy fillets packed in oil, drained and finely chopped
2 teaspoons yellow mustard
2 tablespoons lemon juice
Kosher salt and freshly ground black pepper
1 head Boston lettuce, leaves separated, washed, and dried
2 tablespoons finely chopped parsley

1. Blanch the green beans in lightly salted boiling water until crisp-tender and bright green. Transfer the beans to a bowl of ice water and chill. Drain well and slice into 1-inch lengths.
2. In a bowl, combine the onions, celery, horseradish, olive oil, anchovies, mustard, and lemon juice. Mix well.
3. Add the seitan to the salad. Add the green beans. Toss well and season with salt and pepper.
4. Chill the salad for 1 hour to allow the flavors to marry.
5. To serve: Line each of 4 plates with several leaves of Bibb lettuce. Spoon the salad over the lettuce and sprinkle with chopped parsley.

Pan-Roasted Tofu Steaks with Lemon and Thyme

Serves 4

This delectable, easy-to-prepare dish is packed with protein and zesty flavors. For a sweet, crunchy counterpoint, lightly sauté some julienned vegetables in the pan after you've browned the tofu.

1/2 packed cup chopped fresh mint leaves
3 tablespoons freshly squeezed lemon juice (from about 1 large lemon)
Finely grated zest of 1 lemon
2 large garlic cloves, mashed through a press
1 1/2 teaspoons kosher salt
1 teaspoon red pepper flakes
Two 14-ounce blocks extra-firm tofu, cut into eight 1/2-inch-thick steaks
1/2 cup extra virgin olive oil

1. Make the marinade: In a bowl, whisk together the mint, lemon juice and zest, garlic, salt, and pepper flakes. Whisking constantly, drizzle in the olive oil. Place the marinade in a 1-gallon resealable plastic bag.
2. Place the tofu in the bag with the marinade and refrigerate for up to 4 hours, turning once halfway through.
3. Heat the olive oil in a large cast iron skillet over high heat for several minutes.
4. Lift the tofu from the marinade, pat it gently with a paper towel, and lay it in the pan. Reserve the marinade.
5. Cook for 5 minutes, then reduce the heat to medium and continue to cook until the tofu is golden brown on the bottom, about 5 more minutes. Flip the tofu and cook until browned on the second side, 6 to 8 more minutes.
6. Transfer the tofu to a plate. Pour the oil out of the pan and add the reserved marinade. Stir and simmer for a few seconds, scraping up the browned bits from the bottom of the pan, then pour over the tofu.

Crispy Tofu Mushroom Phyllo Turnovers

Serves 4

A perfect first course to serve at the start of a Mediterranean-style meal, these savory delights are packed with flavor but low in fat.

1 tablespoon extra virgin olive oil
8 ounces mushrooms, finely chopped
1 medium onion, finely chopped (about 1 cup)
3 garlic cloves, minced
Sea salt or kosher salt
1 tablespoon Dijon mustard
1 tablespoon light miso
1 1/2 tablespoons lemon juice
16 ounces firm tofu, mashed with a fork
1 pound baby spinach
Freshly ground black pepper
1 pound phyllo
Vegetable oil or melted butter substitute for brushing the phyllo

1. Preheat the oven to 400 degrees F. In a 10- to 12-inch sauté pan, warm the oil over medium-high heat. Add the mushrooms, onions, garlic, and a pinch of salt. Sauté until the vegetables have softened, about 10 minutes. Add the mustard, miso, lemon juice, and tofu. Stir to combine and simmer for 2 to 3 minutes. Transfer the contents of the pan to a mixing bowl.
2. Steam the spinach over high heat in an inch of water until it wilts, 1 to 2 minutes. Drain and cool under cold running water. Squeeze the spinach dry and chop fine. Add the spinach to the mushroom mixture. Allow the mixture to cool before proceeding.
3. Brush your work surface lightly with oil. Stack 2 sheets of phyllo on the oiled work surface, with a shorter edge facing you. Brush the top sheet with oil. Layer on 2 more sheets and brush with more oil. Repeat once more, for a total of 6 sheets. Cut the rectangle in half lengthwise (the short ends are still facing you). Repeat until you have assembled four 6-layer stacks of phyllo.
4. Mound of the tofu mixture filling in the lower left corner of one rectangle, leaving a border of at least 1 inch. Fold the bottom right corner diagonally over the filling. Lift the filled triangle from the bottom left corner and flip it over so that it remains flush with the left side. Now fold the bottom left corner of the filled triangle diagonally over so that it is flush with the right side. Flip the filled triangle over, so that the end is sealed underneath. Gently place the package seam side down on a rimmed baking sheet. Repeat this with the remaining phyllo.
5. Brush the tops of the triangles with oil. Bake until crisp and golden, 20 to 25 minutes.

TOFU RAGÙ WITH EGGPLANT TIMBALE AND FRESH PEA PUREE

Rich, creamy, and wildly flavorful, this meatless substitute is as delicious as the veal-based version. Serve this the same way, with fresh pea puree (recipe on page 209), and pass warm pita wedges to use as sauce spoons!

1 small eggplant (8 to 10 ounces)
Vegetable oil
1/2 cup all-purpose flour
8 ounces firm tofu, cut into 1/2-inch cubes
Kosher salt and freshly ground black pepper
1 tablespoon extra virgin olive oil
1/4 cup finely chopped onion
1/2 cup finely chopped celery
1/2 cup finely chopped carrot
1 teaspoon peeled, finely chopped fresh ginger
1 teaspoon finely chopped thyme
1 garlic clove, finely chopped
1 tablespoon soy sauce
1/2 cup dry white wine
1/2 cup vegetable stock

1. Preheat the oven to 400 degrees F. Trim the ends from the eggplant. Peel away 1/2-inch wide strips of skin. Cut lengthwise into eight 1/4-inch-thick slices.

2. Reserve 2 teaspoons of the flour for the ragù and spread the rest on a plate. Press each side of the eggplant slices lightly in the flour. Shake off excess.

3. Place a medium skillet over medium-high heat. Add vegetable oil to the depth of 1/2 inch. When the oil is hot, add the eggplant and fry for 1 to 2 minutes per side, until golden brown and tender. Transfer the eggplant to a paper-towel-lined plate to drain. Season with salt and pepper.

4. Make the ragù: Heat the olive oil in an 8- to 10-inch skillet over medium heat until hot. Add the vegetables, thyme, and garlic and sauté 2 minutes. Remove from the heat.

5. Dust the tofu with flour and season with a pinch of salt and pepper. Add the tofu to the vegetables, turn up the heat, and sauté 2 minutes until lightly browned.

6. Add the wine and stock and simmer 3 to 4 minutes, until the liquid has reduced and the veal is tender. Remove from the heat and set aside.

7. Assemble the timbales: Line two 8-ounce soufflé molds or ramekins each with 4 slices of eggplant, draping the eggplant over the sides. Make a layer of diced tomatoes on the bottom of each mold and fill up with tofu ragú. Fold the sides of the eggplant over the ragù.

8. Transfer the molds to a shallow roasting pan. Place the roasting pan on a rack in the middle of the oven and pour boiling water around the molds to come halfway up their sides. Bake for 10 minutes.

9. Run a thin knife blade or spatula around the inside of each mold to loosen the eggplant. Invert the timbales onto two plates. Spoon the pea puree around the timbales and serve immediately.

213

DESSERTS

CARAMELIZED APPLE CREAM PUFFS
WITH YOGURT SAUCE

This very grown-up, velvety version of everyone's favorite candied apple is an elegant way to end any celebration. The crème chantilly, thick pastry cream, and yogurt sauce are all very useful recipes for your dessert arsenal.

Four 3 1/2 x 6-inch pieces frozen puff pastry
1 apple, such as Gala or Golden Delicious
1 teaspoon butter
2 teaspoons brown sugar
2 walnut halves, broken into coarse pieces
3 tablespoons orange juice
Crème chantilly (see below)
Yogurt sauce (see below)
Raspberries and confectioner's sugar for garnish

1. Preheat the oven to 350 degrees F. Lay the pastry on a lightly floured surface. Cut out eight 3-inch rounds. Discard the scraps.
2. Transfer the pastry rounds to an ungreased baking sheet and bake for 15 minutes, until golden brown. Transfer the pastry to a rack to cool.
3. Peel and core the apple and cut into 8 equal wedges. Cut each wedge crosswise into 3 pieces.
4. Place the butter, walnuts, and brown sugar in an 8-inch skillet. Turn the heat on high and cook 1 minute, until the sugar melts and the butter is bubbling. Add the apple and sauté, stirring, for 1 minute. Stir in the orange juice and boil 30 seconds. Transfer to a bowl and set aside to cool. Break up the apple with a fork to form a rough chunky puree.
5. Slice each pastry round in half horizontally for 2 disks. Spoon 2 heaping tablespoons of crème chantilly on the center of 4 of the pastry rounds. Spoon 2 heaped tablespoons of apple over the cream and top with pastry rounds to form 4 sandwiches.
6. Place a pastry on each of 4 plates. Spoon a crescent of yogurt sauce around each pastry. Dust with confectioner's sugar. Garnish the plates with raspberries and serve.

For the crème chantilly:
1/4 recipe Thick Pastry Cream (see below)
1/2 cup heavy cream

Place the pastry cream in a food processor and puree until smooth. In a separate bowl whisk the cream to soft peaks. Add the whipped cream to the pastry cream and pulse to combine.

For the thick pastry cream:
2 cups whole milk
1/2 cup sugar
2 teaspoons vanilla extract
Three 2-inch strips orange peel
Three 2-inch strips lemon peel
3 large eggs
2/3 cup all-purpose flour
1/8 teaspoon kosher salt

1. Combine the milk, 1/4 cup sugar, vanilla, and citrus peels in a medium saucepan and set over high heat. When the milk approaches a boil, remove the pan from the heat.
2. Whisk the eggs in a bowl. Sift the remaining 1/4 cup sugar, flour, and salt into the eggs and beat until smooth and fluffy.
3. Add 1/2 cup of the hot milk into the egg mixture and whisk to combine. Pour the egg mixture into the pan with the remaining hot milk. Cook over medium heat, beating with a rubber spatula or wooden spoon until it turns satiny smooth and pulls away from the sides, about 4 minutes. The cream will reach a temperature of 160 degrees F when it is done.
4. Spread the cream between 2 sheets of parchment paper and set aside until cool and firm.

For the yogurt sauce:
2 tablespoons whole-milk yogurt
3 mint leaves, finely chopped
Pinch of fleur de sel or sea salt

Mix the yogurt, mint, and salt in a dish and refrigerate until ready to serve.

CREMA CATALANA

Serves 4

The classic combination of fruit and subtle coffee essence dances on your tongue in this sublime light dessert. Make this with the ripest nectarine you can find; the result will be out of this world.

1/4 cup plus 1 teaspoon sugar
1 tiny pinch espresso powder
1 egg plus 2 egg yolks
1/2 cup whole milk
1/2 cup heavy cream
1 teaspoon butter and 1 tablespoon sugar for the ramekins
1/2 large ripe nectarine, sliced into 4 even wedges
Confectioner's sugar for serving

1. Preheat oven to 225 degrees F. Combine the sugar, espresso powder, egg, and egg yolks in a mixer. Beat at high speed for 3 minutes or until pale yellow and thick. Lower the speed to medium. Add the milk and cream and mix to combine.
2. Lightly butter four 4-ounce ramekins and dust the bottom and sides of each ramekin with sugar. Place a wedge of nectarine in each ramekin and top with cream. Reserve the leftover cream. Transfer the ramekins to a baking pan and place on a rack in the middle of the oven. Gently pour boiling water around the ramekins to come halfway up the sides.
3. Bake for 15 minutes, until the foam has subsided from the cream. Gently spoon the reserved cream into the ramekins. Bake 1 hour and 15 minutes, until golden brown and barely firm, with a slight jiggle in the center. Cool on a wire rack. Serve dusted with confectioner's sugar.

ROASTED FIGS
WITH FROMAGE BLANC AND RED WINE SAUCE

Serves 4

Succulent, ripe figs are the perfect healthy foil for decadent fromage blanc in this delicious, classic Tuscan-style dessert. Use the freshest, highest-quality figs you can find. If you prefer vanilla ice cream (soy or dairy) to fromage blanc, simply substitute it.

2 heaping tablespoons Rapadura (natural evaporated cane juice crystals)
*   or brown sugar*
2 cups fruity red wine such as merlot
1 tablespoon butter
4 large mint leaves
6 large ripe black mission figs, cut in half
4 tablespoons fromage blanc or mascarpone

1. Heat the sugar in a small saucepan over medium heat for 1 to 2 minutes, until it begins to melt. Add the wine and simmer 12 to 15 minutes until it has reduced to 3 tablespoons and coats the back of a spoon. Remove the pan from the heat.
2. Melt the butter in an 8- to 10-inch skillet over medium heat. Add the mint and cook for 20 seconds. Raise the heat to high. Add the figs and sauté for 2 minutes, turning the figs until they are lightly caramelized and the butter is golden brown.
3. Arrange the figs on plates and drizzle the sauce over and around the figs. Place a scoop of fromage blanc aside the figs and garnish with a mint leaf.

Stacy's Kiss (Sensational, Sexy, "I can't believe it's soy" Panna Cotta)

Serves 4

Silky and melt-in-your-mouth luscious, this surprising soy version of traditional panna cotta will astonish your guests. This dish has become my signature dessert-it's a cause for celebration, and one that my guests look forward to over and over again. Make sure that you use whole soy milk and the highest-quality vanilla bean powder you can find: the result is spectacular.

3 cups vanilla soy milk
Finely grated zest of 1 lemon
Finely grated zest of 1 orange
1 1/2 tablespoons sugar
1 1/2 teaspoons kosher powdered gelatin
1/8 teaspoon ground vanilla bean powder
Fresh raspberries for garnish
Pareve *chocolate for garnish*

1. Combine the soy milk, citrus zests, sugar, gelatin, and vanilla powder in a medium saucepan. Whisk over medium heat until it reaches a boil. Turn off the heat and set aside to cool until lukewarm.
2. Pour Stacy's Kiss into 4 chilled martini glasses and refrigerate until set. Serve topped with fresh berries and shaved *pareve* chocolate.

Chocolate Mousse with Strawberry Tartar

Serves 4

In this velvety-smooth favorite, heavenly strawberry complements earthy chocolate. The key here is making sure your chocolate is of the highest quality: we love Scharffen Berger, an artisanal brand produced in northern California. If you can't find it, simply use the finest chocolate available.

1 1/2 cups heavy cream
18 ripe strawberries, hulled and sliced into 1/4 inch cubes
1 teaspoon lemon juice
1/2 cup milk
1 egg yolk
1 tablespoon plus 1 teaspoon sugar
6 ounces bittersweet chocolate, finely chopped
10 unsalted pistachios, roughly chopped (about 2 tablespoons)

1. Place 1 cup of cream in a bowl and refrigerate.
2. Toss the strawberries with lemon juice and refrigerate.
3. Combine the remaining 1/2 cup cream and milk in a heavy saucepan.
4. Place the egg yolk and sugar in a bowl and whisk until the sugar dissolves. Add the chocolate.
5. Bring the milk and cream to a boil. Pour the hot milk-cream mixture slowly into the chocolate mixture and whisk until smooth.
6. Pour chocolate mixture back into the saucepan. Whisking constantly, cook over medium heat until it reaches 120 degrees F. Transfer the chocolate to a bowl and chill.
7. Whip the 1 cup chilled cream to firm peaks. Fold the cream into the chocolate in three batches until no streaks remain. Transfer the mousse to a pastry bag fitted with a 1/2-inch star tip. Refrigerate the mousse for 30 minutes until firm.
8. To serve: Spoon the strawberries in a line down the center of each plate and sprinkle with chopped pistachios. Pipe the mousse into 1-inch stars alongside the strawberries.

Apricot Agrodolce

In Italian, *agrodolce* means "sweet and sour," and anything prepared that way generally provides a refreshing edge to a meal, either as a palate cleanser or to cut through a meal's richness. However it's used, though, it is invariably low in fat, big in flavor, and simply delicious.

2 tablespoons plus 1 teaspoon butter substitute
1/2 cup plus 2 teaspoons sugar
One 2-inch piece cinnamon stick
3 tablespoons sherry vinegar
3 tablespoons water
6 fresh apricots, quartered
1 bay leaf
1 tablespoon Grand Marnier or orange liqueur
4 apricot pits, smashed with meats reserved
Vanilla soy ice cream or raspberry sorbet

1. Combine 1 teaspoon butter substitute, 1/2 cup sugar, and cinnamon stick in an 8- to 10-inch skillet. Cook undisturbed over medium-high heat until the sugar has melted and turned pale gold, about 4 minutes. Remove the skillet from the heat.
2. Carefully pour the sherry and water into the sugar. The sugar will bubble violently and seize up—that is okay. Return the skillet to medium-low heat and stir until the sugar melts, another 1 to 2 minutes. Transfer the syrup to a small dish.
3. Place 2 teaspoons sugar and 2 tablespoons butter substitute in a medium skillet. Cook over medium heat until the butter melts.
4. Add the apricots and bay leaf. Sauté until lightly browned, 1 to 2 minutes. Add the Grand Marnier and simmer 30 seconds. Remove the skillet from the heat and discard the bay leaf.
5. Arrange 6 apricot slices on each of 4 plates. Spoon the sauce over and around the apricots. Sprinkle the apricots with the chopped meat from the apricot kernels. Serve with a scoop of vanilla soy ice cream or raspberry sorbet.

Apple Granita
with Yogurt and Granola

Forget nuts and twigs: granola is not just for breakfast anymore! Combined with an icy cool apple granita and served in a chilled martini glass, this dessert is the height of luxury, elegance, flavor, and health ... all rolled into one spectacular treat.

1/2 cup freshly squeezed lemon juice
8 large tart green apples with skin, cored and chopped
4 teaspoons sugar
1 cup low-fat yogurt
1 cup of your favorite granola

1. Chill 4 martini glasses in the freezer. Combine the lemon juice and apples in a food processor and process to a smooth puree.
2. Using a rubber spatula, press the puree through a fine sieve into a bowl and whisk in the sugar.
3. Transfer the puree to a shallow pan and freeze until firm. Scrape into crystals, freeze another 30 minutes, and scrape again.
4. Place 2 tablespoons of yogurt into each martini glass. Spoon 1/4 cup of the granita into each glass and top with 2 tablespoons of yogurt, then top the yogurt with the remaining granita. Sprinkle with granola and serve.

218

A Billionaire's Sin: Rich Chocolate Cake

Serves 6

There is no dessert lover in the world who doesn't swoon at the idea of the richest, most sinful chocolate cake they can find. My take on this classic chocolate torte is dense, incredibly rich, and so decadent that you'd never believe it was healthy! (Shhh ... don't tell anyone!) Top it with fresh berries, or serve it au naturel.

6 tablespoons butter
3 ounces bittersweet chocolate, finely chopped
2 tablespoons sugar plus additional for whipped cream
2 egg yolks
2 whole eggs
2 tablespoons flour
1/4 cup heavy cream, whipped and sweetened to taste
Confectioner's sugar for dusting

1. Preheat the oven to 350 degrees F. Melt the butter in a small saucepan over medium heat. Remove the pan from the heat and stir in the chocolate until smooth.
2. In a bowl combine the sugar, egg yolks, and whole eggs. Whisk until the sugar is dissolved. Stir in the chocolate and fold in the flour.
3. Butter and sugar six 4-ounce ramekins. Spoon the batter into the ramekins. Bake for 12 minutes. Remove the ramekins to a to a cooling rack for 5 minutes.
4. To serve: Run a thin knife around the inside of each ramekin to loosen the cakes. Turn the cakes onto plates and garnish with a dollop of freshly whipped cream and a dusting of confectioner's sugar.

Tiramisù

Serves 4

Leave it to the romantic Italians: on the one hand, the name of this dish translates from the Italian to "pick-me-up" (doubtless thanks to the coffee). On the other hand, it can be interpreted to mean that what you're about to eat is like a stairway to heaven: robustly flavored, sinfully good, and surprisingly healthy!

2 tablespoons sugar
2 egg yolks
2 tablespoons heavy cream
2 1/2 ounces mascarpone cheese
1 cup freshly brewed coffee
1 tablespoon sweet marsala wine
12 ladyfingers
2 mint leaves
Unsweetened cocoa powder for dusting

1. Chill 4 martini glasses. Combine sugar and egg yolks in a stand mixer and whip at medium speed for 2 to 3 minutes, until pale and foamy. Add the mascarpone and mix briefly until smooth.
2. In a chilled bowl, whip the cream to soft peaks. Fold the cream into cheese mixture. Cover and refrigerate for 20 minutes.
3. Break the ladyfingers in half. Dip 2 pieces of ladyfinger into the coffee for a moment, until the surface of the cookie is moist but the inside is still firm. Lay the dipped cookies in the bottom of a chilled martini glass. Place 1 tablespoon of the mascarpone cream over the cookies. Dip 2 halves of ladyfingers briefly into the coffee and lay over the cream, and repeat 1 more time, alternating with cream and finishing with a dollop of cream. Repeat with the remaining glasses. Refrigerate until serving time.
4. Top each serving with a mint leaf and a dusting of unsweetened cocoa powder.

"Not knowing when the dawn will come, I open every door."

—EMILY DICKINSON

Acknowledgments

First and foremost, I would like to thank my darling husband for his unwavering support and loving kindness. As my muse, his inspiration and accomplishments motivate me to do far more for and in the world and for myself on a daily basis. I love you.

My heartfelt thanks to Amedeo M. Turello for his creativity, vision, and friendship. His directorship ability and multifaceted talent put him on top with the best in the fashion photography business. Rosanna Trinchese and Roberto Rosini, your passion for making me glamorous will be with me forever. Johanna Rossi, I thank you for your firm attention to detail, and for making this the most beautiful book possible.

Thank you to Quentin Bacon for making my recipes look mouthwateringly delicious; and to Peter Berley for putting my home recipes down on paper, and to George Dolce and his associate, Elisabet der Nederlanden, for their spectacular food styling. Joe Mayer and his associate Chris White did a stunning job with the floral arrangements and food props, and I am forever grateful for their help. Brandon Espanosa's help with the beautiful flowers was also much appreciated.

To Chethan Ramchandran with kind thanks for your patience and business acumen: I couldn't have finished this marathon without you.

My heartfelt thanks to bestselling author and internationally recognized heart doctor Dean Ornish for his inspiration and fabulous heart-healthy ideas for keeping my recipes delicious, kosher, and always heart-healthy. And to Dr. Melina Jampolis, for keeping us on track, inspiring us to be healthy, and for teaching us that eating well and maintaining good health are not mutually exclusive. Your help has been invaluable.

My sincere thanks to Master Sommelier Catherine Fallis for her expert wine pairing; to Peggy and Fred Furth of Chalk Hill Winery; and to Maria Ellen of Petroni Vineyards for her luscious grape garden (and heart-healthy brownies for the team!).

I thank Jessica Kaye for all of her valuable literary advice. Jessica, your friendship and expertise have been so appreciated!

To Jerry Ganz, for being my favorite kosher billionaire with the big heart.

222

Thank you to the Dupree Miller Agency for believing in this project from the word go, to all the Beyond Words team, and to Atria Books/Simon & Schuster for making my vision a published work of art.

Thanks to Elissa Goldheart for her friendship and encouragement every step of the way, and to Anne Cherry for her adorable ways, expert editorial skills, and attention to detail. Your professionalism has been invaluable.

To my dear father for his kindness and for everything he has done for me. Your editing the first draft made it the most complete first draft the publisher had ever seen. And to my grandmothers for their culinary and entertaining inspiration: I love you too.

A special thank you to all the press offices, showrooms, and designers that have worked with us: Akris, Alexander McQueen, Alberta Ferretti, Antonio Marras, Barbara Bui, Blumarine, Carlo Ramello, Celine, Chanel, Christian Dior, Christian Roth, Claudio Merazzi, Diesel, Dolce & Gabbana, DonatellaVersace, Dsquared2, Elie Saab, Emilio Pucci, Ermanno Scervino, Etro, Fendi, Fiona Swarovski, Gaetano Navarra, Gianantonio A. Paladini, Giorgio Armani, Gucci, Jean-Paul Gaultier, Jimmy Choo, Karl Lagerfeld, La Perla, Les Tropeziennes, Louis Vuitton, Marina Poma, Moschino, Philip Treacy, Pollini, Prada, Roberto Cavalli, Valentino, Voyage, Yves Saint Laurent, and the jewelers Chopard, Piaget, Van Cleef & Arpels, Boucheron, and Michael Bruder of Corrupt Design America.

I also wish to thank Larry King, Roberto Cavalli, Lance Armstrong, Sophia Loren, and Donatella Versace for their kind words and generosity of spirit. I am truly honored by their acknowledgment of my work.

Finally, thank you to all the courageous children we have worked with over the years, who continue to motivate and inspire me to do great things in the face of great odds: you will never know how much you mean to me.

—STACY COHEN